RELEASING
HEAVEN
ON EARTH

RELEASING HEAVEN ON EARTH

God's Principles for Restoring the Land

ALISTAIR P. PETRIE

Chosen Books

A Division of Baker Book House Co
Grand Rapids, Michigan 49516

© 2000 by Alistair P. Petrie

Published by Chosen Books
A division of Baker Book House Company
P.O. Box 6287, Grand Rapids, MI 49516-6287

Second printing, April 2001

Printed in the United States of America

Library of Congress Cataloging-in-Publication Data

Petrie, Alistair P., 1950–
    Releasing heaven on earth : God's principles for restoring the land /
    Alistair P. Petrie.
       p. cm.
    Includes bibliographical references and index.
    ISBN 0-8007-9278-5 (pbk.)
    1. Christianity and geography. 2. Spiritual warfare. I. Title.
    BR115.G45 P48 2000

For current information about all releases from Baker Book House, visit our web site:
                http://www.bakerbooks.com

My parents taught me to appreciate the adventure of life.
To them I dedicate this book:
Philip and Margaret Petrie

I also dedicate this book to my mentor,
my colleague and my friend
Dr. C. Peter Wagner

CONTENTS

7

FOREWORD

This book contains one of the most powerful and liberating messages ever to be delivered to the Body of Christ. Why am I making such a broad, sweeping statement? Because it is true.

For years we have taught people to pray over their houses and to cleanse them of occultic objects. We have also told them to dismiss the demonic spirits that might reside in their homes. Since we have had a Western worldview of the issue of land, however, we have perished for lack of knowledge. While we quote Hosea 4:6, we often ignore the beginning of that chapter, which says that God has a controversy with the people of the land for such things as swearing and lying, killing and stealing and committing adultery; therefore, "the land mourns" (Hosea 4:3).

I have not heard many sermons on the subject of the land mourning. It looks strange even as I type it, but it is true. The land *can* mourn. How do I know? Because the Bible says so. It says that the sin of such offenses as lying—which the ordinary person on the street thinks is a small sin, if one at all—causes the land to mourn and to be defiled, and it causes everyone dwelling on that land to waste away. Sin affects even "the beasts of the field," such as cows and sheep, "and the birds of the air and the fish of the sea" (Hosea 4:3). Shocking, but true.

This is why this book contains one of the most important messages that the Church needs to understand today. A couple lives on defiled land and wonders why their perfectly sound marriage starts breaking up when they move into their new house. Others move their businesses to new locations, where the land is defiled by the sin of previous owners, and wonder why all their financial savvy no longer works. Many times we look for any answer other than a spiritual one.

Many different people teach on this subject, and they are all excellent. But I have been anticipating this book by Alistair Petrie for a long time because he probably has more spiritual understanding of the subject of stewardship of the land than anyone I know.

Some of the material in this book is so cutting edge that the Body of Christ was not ready for it even five years ago. This particularly applies in the area of ley lines. I first learned about ley lines in England in 1987. Since that time we have prayed over these lines of occultic power and seen amazing results.

Why do I think now is the time for this book? The Body of Christ has reached an overall maturity level in understanding spiritual warfare and prophetic intercession. They will apply these principles with great joy and results. Many already have done so, with astounding results.

In 1990 one of the first questions I asked a group of leaders, whom we now know as the Spiritual Warfare Network, was, "Do you think that the actual land can be healed?" We know that the answer is yes.

My husband, Mike, and I consider Alistair Petrie to be a man of the highest integrity. Alistair has the best Scottish humor and loves a good laugh. In addition, he loves God's earth and has revelation knowledge that will blow those of us who have had a Western worldview right out of the water. Great job, Alistair! I foresee this book will cause a huge release of souls for the Kingdom and the blessing of God on our houses and land. Turn these pages slowly with pen in hand. God is getting ready to change your life!

Dr. Cindy Jacobs
Co-Founder, Generals of Intercession
Colorado Springs, Colorado

ACKNOWLEDGMENTS

as he finished that book yet?" I seem to have heard this question for the last several years. I have so many people to thank for their encouragement and patience during the years that God has been processing this work in my life. In particular my dear wife, Marie, and my sons, Michael and Richard, deserve a huge medal of thanks. They have been incredible.

To C. Peter Wagner and Cindy Jacobs, my thanks for your ongoing encouragement and inspiration.

To my former parish of Brentwood Anglican Chapel, Brentwood Bay, British Columbia, Canada, my thanks for all your prayers and encouragement over the years. To the board of Joshua Connection Canada, you have been wonderful.

To those who have interceded and prayed for me in various parts of the world, my heartfelt thanks.

To Helen Thornton, who has labored diligently and willingly over many years, and who has done all the typing of the initial manuscript, thank you for the stewardship of your time, labor and love. To her husband, Errol, your support has been invaluable.

To my mother and father, thanks again for everything.

Love and blessings,
A.P.P.

INTRODUCTION

Having been a pastor since 1976, I have preached and taught many times on the subject of stewardship. Only in more recent years, however, have I begun to see the significant relationship between stewardship and the familiar words of 2 Chronicles 7:14: "If my people, who are called by my name, will humble themselves and pray and seek my face and turn from their wicked ways, then will I hear from heaven and will forgive their sin *and will heal their land*" (emphasis added).

Traditionally the Church has understood stewardship in terms of "time, talent and treasure." But when we view it as our responsibility and care for everything God has entrusted to His people, then we examine the stewardship of land, as well as the theology of land, with fresh insight.

When referring to the theology of land, we are speaking of the relationship between God and land—that is, how land reflects the character, nature, goodness and justness of God, especially through the lives of those who live and work on the land. This is a recurring theme throughout the Old Testament. If, as 2 Chronicles 7:14 suggests, land does require healing, then we need to determine how this is undertaken by us as stewards of the land, and how such healing is viewed in Scripture.

The last several years of my life and ministry have been an extraordinary journey of discovery *connecting the stewardship and healing of land with the release of evangelism on that land, resulting in the extension of the Church and overall growth in the Kingdom of God.* This book is a description of that journey—one that has revolutionized my understanding of ministry.

We will cover three main sections: first, a review of traditional biblical stewardship, helping us develop an understanding of this ministry that affects every aspect of human experience on the land. What we do on the land has an extraordinary cause-and-effect impact on our relationship with God as His stewards. As a result we need to understand God's perspective on land, and why He views any form of sin that takes place on the land as a serious issue. When it comes to land, He is a "jealous" God (Joel 2:18).

In the second section we will see the various ways in which man's activity on the land can result in its defilement, based on four major categories of fallen stewardship revealed in Scripture. Then we will examine four main areas of judgment that actually affect the land as a consequence of our sin, thus providing a backdrop for a study of strongholds and bondages and the means by which these issues gain access to both people and communities.

The third section provides insight into the cleansing and healing of land, and the seven areas of blessing that are released, according to Scripture, when land is properly stewarded and healed. This will help us look at practical ways that entire communities and cities can be diagnosed, revealing the sources of any adverse spiritual conditions, how these can be reversed and how changes at every level of community life can be retained.

We will examine what faithful stewardship of the land involves, and will look at some current examples of community transformation, all of which give testimony to the blessings of God on His people once the land is healed.

The ultimate goal of this book: to address the issue referred to in 2 Corinthians 4:4: "The god of this age has blinded the minds of unbelievers, so that they cannot see the light of the gospel of the glory of Christ, who is the image of God." I have written this book in the belief that people blind to the Gospel of Christ can have their hearts, minds and eyes opened to Jesus Christ when the issues that have previously held them in spiritual darkness, whether individual or corporate, are revealed and removed.

The understanding of the Body of Christ in our position as stewards of the land, and our employment as stewards, prepares the way of the Lord for His visitation, habitation and transformation in our lives, our cities and our nations.

The Rev. Dr. Alistair P. Petrie
British Columbia, Canada

Part 1

FOUNDATIONS OF BIBLICAL STEWARDSHIP

ONE

THE CALL TO BE STEWARDS

ormally when the average churchgoing Christian hears the word *stewardship* mentioned in church circles, he or she thinks in terms of Stewardship Sunday and the church's need of funds. A certain stigma is attached to the word *stewardship*, and we tend to avoid its challenging overture.

The English word *steward* comes from an Old English root word, *stigweard*, which referred to a person who handled the property or possessions belonging to somebody else. In other words, a steward is someone responsible for somebody else's goods and chattels. Genesis 1:28 clearly describes this understanding of stewardship:

> Be fruitful and increase in number; fill the earth and subdue it. Rule over the fish of the sea and the birds of the air and over every living creature that moves on the ground.

Here is a vivid picture of humanity being responsible for, or managing, God's property and possessions.

This is one of the very first directives given to man by God: "The LORD God took the man and put him in the Garden of Eden to work it and take care of it" (Genesis 2:15). The Hebrew word *shamar* used in this verse has many meanings: to hedge around something, to keep, to guard, to watch as a watchman, to protect. That is our stewardship responsibility—nothing less than *to keep the land*.

Stewardship, then, is a divine principle emphasizing our accepting responsibility for possessions entrusted to us by somebody else, more than our giving away our possessions. This is our personal and corporate call to be stewards of the Kingdom of God. Putting it simply, stewardship speaks of management.

Stewards with a Purpose

Environmentalism and the study of ecology have taught us that good stewardship of the earth produces positive results, whereas poor stewardship results in devastation. Environmental groups like Greenpeace are loud proponents of this principle. Thomas Kelshaw puts it this way: "Stewards have *power* over certain things, but it is clear that this is a power to *care,* or take *care* of things. Stewardship means being answerable to God for our use of these *powers.*"[1]

Indeed, biblical stewardship teaches us that we are responsible to God to manage and care for His resources, remembering that they always belong to Him and never to us. This was the arrangement in the Garden of Eden. Only after sin entered the picture and man became estranged from God did he begin struggling against thorns and thistles while trying to produce fruit from the ground. Subsequently man began to hoard what he gained, and forgot he was but a tenant of God's resources in this world.

Leviticus 25 provides insight into man's relationship with the land on God's terms. In verse 23, for example, God says, "The land must not be sold permanently, because the land is mine and you are but aliens and my tenants." We are, again, caretakers, managers and occupiers, looking after all that God has given us. Kelshaw reminds us that "God is a giving God who calls us into being a giving people. We are stewards of God's grace, not masters of His bounty."[2]

Being managers of God's stewardship is a concept found in both Old and New Testaments. In the New Testament the perspective of stewardship as management is found in the use of the Greek word *oikonomos*, which means "manager," and is used in the Parable of the Steward.

The context of this parable in Luke 12 concerns the watchfulness of the steward for the return of the master, and includes the responsibility charged to that steward, who looks after the household during the master's absence. This person, an *oikonomos*, is given the necessary money with which to pay the bills, feed the servants and maintain the household. In Luke 12:42 Jesus refers to the one who is faithful and wise in this responsibility as a "manager." In the next verse He describes this same faithful manager as a "servant," using the Greek word *doulos*, meaning, literally, "slave."

We learn from this parable that the manager of the master's property never ceases to be the servant of the master, but he performs faithfully and responsibly the task appointed him in stewardship. Kelshaw puts it this way: "He is still a slave, but now is a slave with responsibilities. So it is with us—we are slaves to Jesus Christ, because as Christians we have been bought (redeemed) and have been given responsibility in the household of God. We, too, are accountable."[3]

We are, therefore, stewards on a divine mission.

Time, Talent and Treasure

One of the consequences of our fallen nature is that mankind wants to hoard possessions, illustrating a lack of trust in God's ability to provide for us every day. This is an issue we see developing throughout the Old Testament, from the time of the Fall in the Garden of Eden. In the early stages of the wilderness years, God wanted to instill this principle in the hearts of His people. He said to Moses:

> "I will rain down bread from heaven for you. The people are to go out each day and gather enough for that day. In this way I will test them and see whether they will follow my instructions. On the sixth day they are to prepare what they bring in, and that is to be twice as much as they gather on the other days."
>
> Exodus 16:4–5

If the people gathered more than the required allocation on a particular day, the excess became moldy.

Whether it is manna or money, we try to increase our possessions because we think they express what we are. We often view money as an investment rather than a cash flow, because it can represent power, decision-making, our sense of security. But it also reveals the state of our souls, because we often become what we own. The philosophy of the world is that if we possess little, then we can be considered worthless, while those considered worthy are the ones who have possessions and treasures. In the eyes of the world they possess power. In the words of the familiar bumper sticker, *He who dies with the most toys wins!*

All this is a form of stewardship, albeit one based on self-interest and the desire to accrue possessions. As a result, when Stewardship Sunday arrives, we are seen to be releasing some of *our* possessions into the church's coffers—giving of *our* time, talent and treasure. This, as we have seen, is a limited understanding of stewardship.

None of us is in a position to offer God a proportion of what He already owns! As the first verse of the hymn by Bishop William W. How (1858) puts it,

We give Thee but Thine own,
Whate'er the gift may be;
All that we have is Thine alone,
A trust, O Lord, from Thee.

Everything Belongs to God

According to biblical stewardship, God calls us to manage all that belongs to Him. We are called to servanthood, entrustment and final accounting. It is not *our* time, talent and treasure in question, but *God's*. We are stewards of all He has entrusted to us. As the psalmist reminds us, "The earth is the LORD's and the fullness thereof, the world and those who dwell therein" (Psalm 24:1, RSV).

Our time, talents and money all belong to God in the first place. He has bequeathed these to us to be invested carefully, so that His Kingdom can be extended through our stewardship of His resources. We learn from Ananias and Sapphira (see Acts 5) to be people of integrity when it comes to our management of His stewardship.

We are to subdue the creation and have dominion over it as representatives of the Creator. We are both *keepers* and *preservers* of creation, caring for it in God's name and on His behalf. The chief Steward is Jesus Christ, our perfect model of stewardship. How we live out our stewardship as individuals and as the corporate Church becomes our expression of faith as we serve God by serving the world and other people.

It is clear by now that this extends well beyond the subject of money. Stewardship is neither a season nor a program; rather, it is a complete way of life. Bruce C. Birch, former Professor of Old Testament at Wesley Theological Seminary in Washington, D.C., reminds us of this biblical perspective:

> ... Caring for all of creation is highlighted in the theme of creation in the image of God (Gen. 1:26). Here the Bible affirms

25

the unique and precious quality of every person, male and female, as one created in the image of God, but this is not just a
gift. It is also a responsibility. To be created in the image of God
is a gift that brings with it the responsibility to care for God's
creation (cf. Gen. 1:28, 2:15). It was a practice of ancient kings
to erect images of themselves to represent their sovereignty in
the far-flung corners of their empires. The biblical writer has
transferred this metaphor to the divine realm. In Genesis 1,
God, who is truly sovereign over all creation, has chosen to place
the divine image into human beings as the representatives, not
of some inherent human right of our own to exploit the creation for our own needs, but as the trustees of God.[4]

There is, therefore, an influence placed within us as God's
stewards that will affect our respective areas of responsibility as
trustees of His creation. This effect can be either positive or
negative, depending on how we carry out our responsibility as
God's stewards. This, in turn, can have a significant impact on
the ecology around us.

Down to Earth

In talking about stewardship and ecology, we need to be
"down to earth" in our understanding of this subject. In his
book *The Steward: A Biblical Symbol Come of Age*, Douglas John
Hall states: "The steward is one of the most provocative as well
as historically accessible concepts to contemplate for anyone
who cares about the destiny of our civilization."[5] The bottom
line: Our stewardship becomes an influencing factor in society around us. "Stewardship is the material means," Hall states,
"by which the spiritual end is achieved."[6]

Biblical Christianity would argue that the role of the steward defines our mission as people of God. To quote Hall again,
we need "to evolve a stewardship praxis that is more than a
shadow of the biblical metaphor."[7] Hall points out that the

26

Bible contains some 26 direct references to the terms *steward* or *stewardship*.[8] When a steward truly understands his relationship and identity with the Master, he can have an enormous influence on society, which in turn extends to our stewardship of God's creation (ecology).

The editor of *Earthkeeping in the Nineties: Stewardship of Creation,* Loren Wilkinson, makes an interesting observation on this point:

> This growing awareness of our obligation to the earth . . . places Christians in a difficult position. On the one hand, we affirm that God made the earth, called it good, and directs its course. And we believe that God continues to care for it. The word translated "world" in the New Testament is usually *kosmos,* which means, in its broadest sense, "cosmos," the universe. When Christians affirm that God loved the world, and that Christ died for the life of the world, they are speaking not just of humanity, but of the whole planet—indeed, the whole created universe. Thus, of all people, Christians should be concerned for the future health of the planet—both for the narrow "world" of humankind and the broader "earth" of the complex and living ecosphere.[9]

But Western Christendom has not shown a great deal of concern for the world's health—likely due, in large part, to our Western-based worldview. Native North Americans often refer to themselves as "people of the land" or "people of the sea." But those of us with a European background, who are still affected by the thinking of the Enlightenment, do not view things with the same spiritual perspective. Indeed, evangelical Christians often refer to people being saved "out of the world." As Wilkinson states: "That idea has been interpreted by many to be a sort of license to neglect the world in order to care for the soul."[10]

Biblical Christianity, on the other hand, teaches intimate harmony among God, mankind and creation. Ponder the ideal picture of Psalm 104, in which God is portrayed as the cause:

He makes grass grow for the cattle, and plants for man to
cultivate—bringing forth food from the earth: wine that glad-
dens the heart of man, oil to make his face shine, and bread
that sustains his heart. The trees of the LORD are well watered,
the cedars of Lebanon that he planted. There the birds make
their nests; the stork has its home in the pine trees.

Psalm 104:14–17

When God is removed from the relationship between man
and creation, we can construct another Babel. The problem
with groups such as Greenpeace is that the earth itself becomes the object of worship and we forget that, in Wilkinson's words, "not only is the earth the Lord's, but the future is
His as well."[11]

We must at all times worship the Creator and be faithful
stewards of His creation, while at the same time avoiding the
subtle danger of making creation the object of our worship
(see Romans 1:25). As Christians we are called not *out* of the
world, but rather *into* it, in order to make a difference as salt
and light *to* the world. Part of our concern, then, necessitates
dealing with the issues of acid rain, the ozone layer and the
pollution of our environment growing at an alarming rate, as
well as the ensuing issues of war, famine and disease. As long
as we live in this world without being affected by its thinking,
such issues bring us down to earth in the way we apply the
Kingdom of God here in this world.

How do we address these issues as stewards of God's creation and His grace?

Birds, Rocks and Thorns

In order to answer this last question, it may be helpful to
refer to the well-known Parable of the Sower (see Matthew
13). This parable is often referred to as "the parable of the soils,"
which reveal the condition of a person's soul. We may share

28

the good news of Christ, but we need to be aware of birds, rocky places and thorns, all of which, as issues within people's lives, influence their acceptance or rejection of the Gospel. It is easy to see this passage in terms of what I call a "harvest expectancy scale." In other words, our theological interpretation of this parable often gives God a "way out" when reference is made to sowing His Word, since we are aware of hindrances that prevent an effective response. We are not to be overly concerned, therefore, if our evangelism is less fruitful than we would like. That is just the state of life!

The good news of this passage is that some seed does fall on good soil and produce a high return. Nevertheless Jesus ends this passage with a deeper teaching on the issue of the Kingdom of heaven and our ability to see and hear what God is saying.

My family comes from an agricultural background. I learned that in order to prepare for a good harvest, it is necessary to remove as many stones and weeds from the field as possible before sowing the seed. As I have reflected on Matthew 13 over the last several years, I believe God is giving deeper insight into our role as stewards of the land than what is normally taught at seminary. Would it not make sense to remove the spiritual rocks and thorns from a community before the work of evangelism takes place? It would then be a matter of keeping the spiritual birds at bay, once the seed was in place.

If as stewards we are acting on behalf of the owner of the resources of the land, *it would make sense for us to clear the land of whatever impediments exist that might minimize an effective harvest.*

This theme is picked up elsewhere in Scripture: "It will be said: 'Build up, build up, prepare the road! Remove the obstacles out of the way of my people'" (Isaiah 57:14). This admonition includes a statement of building, preparing and removing, as well as God's expectation that this imperative will be undertaken and implemented.

The words are similar to those found in Isaiah 62:10: "Pass through, pass through the gates! Prepare the way for the people.

Build up, build up the highway! Remove the stones. Raise a banner for the nations." Again there is a sense of preparation, of building, of removing stones, implying that, as a result, a banner will be raised for the nations.

Does this suggest there are ways we can pray for the nations of the world through which impediments can be removed on a corporate basis, thus releasing those nations into a deeper sense of God's call and purpose for their existence? Contemporary Church trends indicate that this is indeed the case.

Is it possible that the ecological problems we find in the world today are the fruit of unresolved issues in the land that have never been dealt with properly? Are biblical passages such as Isaiah 57, Isaiah 62 and Matthew 13 challenging our worldview in order that we begin to see issues around us from an entirely different perspective? Are there biblical guidelines that can open up our eyes and ears to this deeper teaching on stewardship of the land, resulting in the land being healed and the people of the land responding to the invitation of the Gospel?

In the era of a new millennium, these are crucial questions with which the Church must wrestle. This book is a response to these questions. Let's look with unveiled eyes and minds at the issues of stewardship and land from the perspective of the Kingdom of God.

TWO

GOD'S PERSPECTIVE ON LAND

 od loves the land. It is, after all, His creation. In the book *Commitment to Conquer* Bob Beckett observes: "In every season, in any place created by God, we find beauty . . . because God has put something of Himself in all creation."[1] Land is important to God because it speaks of Him and reflects His character. God actually cares about the land we walk on!

Beckett identifies 1,717 references to the word *land* in Scripture[2]—more references than to justification by faith, the virgin birth, repentance, baptism and Christ's return.

In *Healing the Land* Winkie Pratney lists the biblical words rendered *land* in the King James Version, first explaining the Old Testament words from the Hebrew, then the New Testament words from the Greek. The Hebrew word *adamh* is used 111 times to describe country, earth, ground; *ezrach*, meaning bay, born (in the land); *erets*, meaning common, country, earth, field, ground, land; *yabbashah*, meaning dry ground (land); and *sadeh*, meaning country, field, ground, land, soil, wild. In the New Testament we find the word *agros*, meaning country, farm, piece of ground, land; *ge*, meaning country, earth(ly), ground, land, world; *xeros*, meaning dry, land, withered; *chora*, meaning coast, country, fields, ground, land, region; and *chorion*, meaning field, land, parcel of ground, place, possession.[3]

Deuteronomy 11:10–12 states:

> The land you are entering to take over is not like the land of Egypt, from which you have come, where you planted your seed and irrigated it by foot as in a vegetable garden. But the land you are crossing the Jordan to take possession of is a land of mountains and valleys that drinks rain from heaven. *It is a land the* LORD *your God cares for;* the eyes of the LORD your God are continually on it from the beginning of the year to its end.

emphasis added

Deuteronomy 28:12 further states:

> The LORD will open the heavens, the storehouse of his bounty, to send rain on your land in season and to bless all the work of your hands. You will lend to many nations but will borrow from none.

Finally Job 12:7–8 states:

> "Ask the animals, and they will teach you, or the birds of the air, and they will tell you; *or speak to the earth, and it will teach you,* or let the fish of the sea inform you."

emphasis added

God uses land, in other words, to state His purpose, direction and desire for the lives of His people. Little wonder He asks us to look after His land so carefully!

God Is Jealous for His Land

Perhaps this helps explain the well-known words of Joel 2:18: "The LORD will be *jealous for his land* and take pity on his people" (emphasis added). Man is the crowning achievement of God's creation.

Genesis 1:26 indicates that man was created in the image of God:

> Then God said, "Let us make man in our image, in our likeness, and let them rule over the fish of the sea and the birds of the air, over the livestock, over all the earth, and over all the creatures that move along the ground."

Thus, while man is part of God's creation, he is given a unique position within it: He is to care for it. Genesis 1:28:

> God blessed them and said to them, "Be fruitful and increase in number; fill the earth and subdue it. Rule over the fish of the sea and the birds of the air and over every living creature that moves on the ground."

The word *subdue* in Hebrew, *kabash*, has a military nuance, meaning "to conquer" or "to take authority or particular responsibility." Man is responsible for God's creation in a unique way. As a wise steward he is to handle with justice and wisdom the issues that come forth from creation. The word for *rule* in Hebrew is *radah*, which means "to conquer." It also carries the implication of redirecting assets like an accountant from one place to another, in order that correct disbursement takes place.

God's love and care for His creation has been placed firmly into the hands of that part of creation made in His very own image. It is important for us to see and understand land from God's perspective, then, and to know why He is jealous for His land.

In his fascinating book *The Land*, Walter Brueggemann explains that "land is not given over to any human agent, but is a sign and function in covenant."[4] God is a God of covenant, Brueggemann points out: "The way to keep the land and power over it is to turn attention from land to Torah. By implication the way to lose land is to be anxious about it, to the neglect of Torah."[5]

When Ahab and Jezebel try to seize Naboth's vineyard and make it their own, Brueggemann explains Ahab's understanding of land as a tradable commodity: "'Give me your vineyard, that I may have it for a vegetable garden, because it is near my house; I will give you a better vineyard for it; or, if it seems good to you, I will give you its value in money' (1 Kings 21:2)."

Brueggemann explains that for Naboth, however, "land is not a tradable commodity, but an inalienable inheritance. 'The LORD forbid that I should give you the inheritance of my fathers. . . . I will not give you the inheritance of my fathers' (1 Kings 21:3–4)." Naboth's land has been held in trust from one generation to another, and he is to steward this land with

> preservation and enhancement of the gift for the coming generations. Naboth is responsible for the land, but is not in control over it. It is the case not that the land belongs to him, but that he belongs to the land. Naboth foresees himself and the land in a covenantal relation, with the relation between the two having a history of fidelity which did not begin with him and will not end with him.[6]

In this line of reasoning, land is seen in the eyes of the Lord as "covenanted community" in which both people and land are intimately connected with God. The people of the Old Testament determined their identity from the land on which they lived and worked, and this in turn reflected the nature and character of God as One with whom they were in covenant relationship. Little wonder God is interested in the way we live and work as His stewards on His land!

The God of Geography and History

With all this in mind, we can now see why Scripture provides some fascinating insights into the way God has developed, organized and situated His people all over the world. As Brueggemann puts it, "Torah exists so that Israel will not forget whose land it is and how it was given to us."[7] The Torah, or the revealed will of God as seen in the Mosaic law and the emerging relationship of God and His people in the Pentateuch, is intimately tied up with obedience to Yahweh and with the honoring of the covenant. "Israel's Torah . . . is . . . interested in care for the land, so that it is never forgotten from whence came the land and to whom it is entrusted and by whom."[8]

Repeatedly Scripture shows the connection between God, people, land and geography, based on the people's attitude and relationship to God at any given time. Here are several examples that graphically outline this relationship between God, land and His people.

In Genesis 9:19 we read that God *scattered* the descendants of the sons of Noah. In Genesis 10:20, 31 He *placed* the ancient peoples and nations in their respective lands. Genesis 11:8–9, the consequence of Babel, refers to God's *scattering* the people at a time when they wished to be autonomous from Him. In Deuteronomy 32:8 we learn that God *establishes* boundaries for people, and Job 12:23 refers to His *enlarging* and *dispersing* nations. Psalm 16:5–6 refers to the psalmist's "lot" (meaning his portion, allocation, destiny or area of responsibility) being made secure. In verse 6 the psalmist refers to the *establishing* of God's boundary lines, meaning His measured portion of responsibility for His people. In Psalm 78:54 we read again of "the border of his holy land." He *allots* lands and *settles* tribes (people groups). Psalm 74:17 points out that God has *established* all the boundaries of land in the world. Isaiah 9:3 and 26:15 refer to God's *increasing the joy* of a nation and *extending its borders*, while Ezekiel 16:26–27 refers to God's *reducing our territory* (influence and stewardship) when we sin.

That Ezekiel passage—a fascinating reference!—indicates clearly that our stewardship influence can be either good or bad; and when it is contrary to God's purposes for His people, He will minimize our effectiveness.

35

In the same vein Lamentations 2:8–9 refers to God's tearing down the wall around the Daughter of Zion, thus removing His protection and identity from within her midst because of her sinfulness, and stretching out a measuring line that can bring judgment and destruction on His people. Isaiah 30:28 refers to God's sifting nations and subduing them, while Isaiah 34:11 refers to His stretching out "the measuring line of chaos and the plumb line of desolation"—a judgment that can affect us territorially due to our sin. Luke 1:51 mentions God scattering those who are proud—again, reducing their influence. According to Jeremiah 1:10 God can even give certain nations the mandate to root out and pull down. To build and to plant other nations—quite an extraordinary calling for any nation to undertake! And Deuteronomy 32:8 indicates that God makes nations to inherit other nations.

Each of these Bible references contains active and intentional involvement on God's part, indicating His geographical and historical jurisdiction over and within the lives of His people. He has the right to such jurisdiction because He is the Lord of the earth. At the same time we need to remember that God's overall desire is to bless nations.

Lord of History, Lord of the Earth

In their book A *Matter of the Heart: Healing Canada's Wounds*, Rudy and Marny Pohl identify "the first biblical pillar" in the relationship between God and people in this way—that "God is the sovereign Lord of history."[9] They refer to Daniel 2:21: "He changes times and seasons; he sets up kings and deposes them"; Psalm 47:8–9, declaring that "God reigns over the nations . . . the kings of the earth belong to God"; and Psalm 33:10–11: "The LORD foils the plans of the nations; he thwarts the purposes of the peoples. But the plans of the LORD stand firm forever, the purposes of his heart through all generations."

36

God is Lord over history, nations, kingdoms and all the peoples of the earth. Jeremiah 10:7 refers to God as "King of the nations," and Psalm 22:28 declares that "dominion belongs to the LORD and he rules over the nations." Finally Proverbs 21:1 states that "the king's heart is in the hand of the LORD; he directs it like a watercourse wherever he pleases." Here again we see God's active intervention and influence on people and nations.

God uses human beings to carry out His plans and purposes for His people, but He is always in control. Whatever happens on His land comes under His ultimate sovereignty. The quality of our stewardship, which God has entrusted to us, determines how He acts toward us and within our lives.

Acts 17:26 states that God determines exactly when and where people live:

> From one man he made every nation of men, that they should inhabit the whole earth; and he determined the times set for them and the exact places where they should live.

The Greek word for *made* is *epoiaysen,* indicating the forming of something—in this case, the forming of humanity into nations. God actually *creates* nations. No nation or government can ever act autonomously from Him. This verse also states that God appoints times and seasons in history for every nation to exist on the earth. The Greek words used here, *horisas* and *prostetagmenous,* imply ordaining and fore-appointing. Combined with the Greek word *kairos,* meaning an appointed time period, these words give the impression that nothing happens on the earth that has not been previously formed in the mind of God (in contrast to His Torah).

This reference also teaches us that God ordains the boundaries of each nation. The Greek word *horothesias* means an exact "limiting place," which comes from the root word *horion,* meaning boundary line, frontier or border. Again this emphasizes God's sovereign control over every nation in the history of creation. Perhaps the simplest explanation for God's being so involved in the physical positioning and destiny of nations is so that they might seek Him and worship Him as their sovereign Lord, and so fulfill His purposes for them as His people. It seems clear from Scripture that nations are given time to seek and find God, but that if they refuse to do this, then He will deal with them accordingly. God loves His nations— and the missionary mandate assigned to the Church is to share His love through Jesus Christ with every nation in the world.

I have read various accounts in recent years of overseas missionaries observing a peculiar phenomenon. People in one part of a community, once witnessed to, may demonstrate little response to the Gospel message; but they may respond quite differently, perhaps even accepting Christ as Savior, in another part of that same physical community. Why are people apparently closed to the Gospel in one area, yet more willing to accept the Gospel only a short distance away?

The reason for this scenario—which has become familiar in recent years in many parts of the world—is a matter of stewardship. Whatever takes place in one part of a community over the years differs from what takes place in another part. The result: *a difference in spiritual climate*. This variance in spiritual climate exists all over the world, in both individuals and nations, and affects people's response to the Gospel.

What is it that gives such variance in the right of occupancy to an area of land? Simply put, it lies in the understanding of our stewardship.

Stewards, People of Influence

A steward, as we have seen, is someone entrusted with the responsibility and care of property. A Christian steward is responsible for God's property. So long as we live in a world estranged from God, however, our stewardship is subject to defilement and therefore requires cleansing. Until this takes place, birds, rocks and thorns—the enemies of the seed in Jesus' parable—block people from entering the land God has prepared for them. Later we will see that a steward is called to reclaim for God the land that is rightfully His, which has been lost through fallen or sinful stewardship.

The steward brings defilement into his life and work in at least three possible ways. First, *by what he does himself.* When Cain killed Abel, for example (see Genesis 4:8), he was immediately estranged in his relationship with God and had to leave God's presence (see verse 16). Furthermore the ground would no longer yield any harvest for him (see verse 12). Cain lost both relationship and stewardship.

Second, the steward is subject to defilement *through how he relates to what others do and say to him, and his subsequent reactions* (anger, hate, murder, sexual sin). Under Delilah's influence Samson broke his vow as a Nazirite and lost his anointing as a judge of the land. Jealousy and anger affected Saul in the way he related to David, and subsequently affected his relationship to God and his reign as king.

There is a third way in which the steward experiences defilement in his life and work, and that is *through inheritance from earlier generations passed on into the present.* Leviticus 26:39–42 gives us some indication of the inheritance of past sin into the present generation. Verse 39 is explicit:

> Those of you who are left [not killed by your enemies] will waste away in the lands of their enemies because of their sins; also because of their fathers' sins they will waste away.

Similarly Deuteronomy 23:2 indicates some form of defilement entering a family lineage for as many as ten generations when one is born from a forbidden marriage or, as the footnote for this verse in several translations suggests, illegitimately. There is a sense in various parts of Scripture in which the people of the present generation are affected by what they inherited from the stewards of former generations. In a well-known prayer, Daniel confesses the sins of his generation as well as the sins of his fathers (Daniel 9:4–14). In chapter 4 we will review the crucial issue of generational sin from a biblical perspective.

When we examine our position as stewards of Christ, it is important to acknowledge who we are, as revealed in Scripture. Deuteronomy 7:6 indicates that we are a holy people, chosen by God to be His. Deuteronomy 5:7–10 teaches that we are not to worship anyone or anything other than the living God.

Indeed, Deuteronomy 5:9 is graphic in its explanation: "I, the LORD your God, am a jealous God, punishing the children for the sin of the fathers to the third and fourth generation of those who hate me." Here again we see that the sin of the past can affect us in the present. It is important for us, therefore, to be expedient in our stewardship responsibility before God so that we do not adversely affect the generation of tomorrow.

In Exodus 19:5–6 God reminds His people that we are His "treasured possession," and that, although the whole earth belongs to Him, we are "a kingdom of priests and a holy nation." The apostle Peter continues this description of our position in Christ:

> You are a chosen people, a royal priesthood, a holy nation, a people belonging to God, that you may declare the praises of him who called you out of darkness into his wonderful light. Once you were not a people, but now you are the people of God. . . .
>
> 1 Peter 2:9–10

Paul also reminds us of our position in Christ: "You died, and your life is now hidden with Christ in God" (Colossians 3:3). In Colossians 1:27 Paul says that to the saints, "God has chosen to make known among the Gentiles the glorious riches of this mystery, which is Christ *in* you, the hope of glory" (emphasis added).

Paul's overall desire in that book is to remind the Colossians of their new nature in Christ. Both the Old and New Testaments teach us this distinctiveness in our relationship with God as His people, His stewards.

Leviticus 20 makes it clear that God did not want His people to walk in the pestilence of earlier inhabitants in the new land He was giving His people. His declaration concerning the way His people must live is clear:

> "You must not live according to the customs of the nations I am going to drive out before you. Because they did all these things, I abhorred them. But I said to you, 'You will possess their land; I will give it to you as an inheritance, a land flowing with milk and honey.' I am the LORD your God, who has set you apart *from the nations.*"

> verses 23–24, emphasis added

Similarly Joshua challenged his people as they took residence in the Promised Land:

> "Throw away the gods your forefathers worshiped beyond the River and in Egypt, and serve the LORD. . . . Choose for yourselves this day whom you will serve. . . . But as for me and my household, we will serve the LORD."

> Joshua 24:14–15

Joshua wanted his people to declare their obedience to Yahweh and to separate themselves from the influence of the cultural background of the idolaters who had lived in the land before them.

Deuteronomy 11:26–28 summarizes God's intention. He stated that His people would be blessed if they obeyed Him, and cursed if they turned away from His unique purpose for them and instead followed the way of other gods. Simply put, good stewardship requires obedience and a living witness as to our position in Christ.

41

Land and Its Defilement

Land takes on characteristics based on what we do on it, both good and bad. Land can be either defiled or blessed by the people who inhabit it. Throughout Scripture we find numerous examples of how the stewards of the day had a distinct effect on their environment.

In Genesis 3:17 we are told that the ground became cursed because of the fallen stewardship of Adam and Eve, and verses 18 and 19 describe the "thorns and thistles" that would now be part of their day-to-day experience as they worked the land.

In looking at Genesis 4 again, we have this account of Abel's blood crying out from the ground following his murder at the hands of his brother, Cain. The ground was describing the nature of the untimely stewardship. Genesis 4:11–12 describes the effect on Cain, who was "driven from the ground" because of the curse placed on him, and we are told that he would "be a restless wanderer on the earth." Concerning this Scripture, Beckett states that

> to be a vagabond means to be homeless, and it is a curse. Moving from place to place leaves one with a desperate feeling of not belonging. Under such circumstances there can be no chance for vision or destiny to take root.[10]

But the ground had been crying out for justice!

Joshua 7 gives another example of defilement on the land due to fallen stewardship. Here we have the account of Achan's sin, in which he deliberately disobeyed God's orders, as issued through Joshua, concerning the total destruction of Jericho. Achan retained some of the plunder, in the form of a beautiful robe and shekels of silver and gold, and hid them in the ground inside his tent. This act is regarded as hiding or burying fetishes, or articles that can be used for idolatrous worship, which may give the demonic realm the right of access in this place.

Due to Achan's sin the area became known as the Valley of Achor. Several Bible versions translate this in footnotes as *the Valley of Trouble.* Again we see a distinct relationship between people's stewardship and the resulting effect on the land and people.

Numbers 13:23–24 describes the spies' exploration of Canaan. The cluster of grapes they cut off was so large that the place it came from was called the Valley of Eshcol, meaning "cluster." Here is an example of a positive effect, in that the fruitfulness of this area described the land as a whole.

By contrast, Acts 1:18–19 explains that the field in which Judas committed suicide was referred to as Akeldama (Field of Blood), describing the characteristic now placed on that field: untimely bloodshed.

Leviticus 18:24–25 warns people against defilement, since land that is defiled must be "punished . . . for its sin," and the people subsequently removed from their positions of work and responsibility ("vomited out" of the land).

Leviticus 18:27–28 makes it clear that the people of an earlier generation were involved in various forms of defilement, which subsequently affected the land, and that similar defilement would cause the land also to "vomit you out."

Leviticus 19:29 describes how land can "be filled with wickedness" due to prostitution. The sin of prostitution, in other words, a form of fallen stewardship, affects the whole of that land area.

Jeremiah 2:7 further clarifies the principle of stewardship:

> "I brought you into a fertile land to eat its fruit and rich produce. But you came and *defiled my land* and made my inheritance detestable."
>
> emphasis added

Perhaps we can understand the implication of the prophet's words more fully in Jeremiah 12:4:

How long will the land lie parched and the grass in every field be withered? Because those who live in it are wicked, the animals and birds have perished.

Pratney quotes Job 31:38, 40: "If my land cries out against me and all its furrows are wet with tears, . . . then let briers come up instead of wheat and weeds instead of barley." The Hebrew word *za'aq*, Pratney points out, is translated by the English words "cries out"—"to shriek from anguish or a sense of danger. It is a distress signal."[11] Then Pratney asks this searching question:

> Is it possible that we live among a hurting creation, literally mourning the sin of mankind? Does the earth itself actually weep over what man in sin is doing to the creation, to each other, to God?[12]

Hundreds of examples throughout Scripture show land taking on the characteristics of either negative or positive stewardship, due to the influence of the people who have lived and worked on that land. Such is the importance of understanding stewardship from God's perspective. We, as His stewards, have an effect, both positive and negative, on the land and environment around us. The quality of our stewardship will always affect whatever environment we are influencing—whether people, churches, cities or nations.

The Foundation and Character of Land

As God's stewards, we are responsible for the defilement or cleansing of the land. This is one of the reasons that, under the present-day discipline of spiritual mapping—in effect, simply understanding the spiritual and physical dynamics of a community from God's perspective, otherwise known as its "spir-

44

itual DNA"—prayer teams and leadership are trying to determine the character of their communities or cities.

This character is composed of vision, traditions, stewardship, culture, social mores and the spirituality of the various people groups that have inhabited the land in past generations. Each community or land area is shaped by these components, and continues to be shaped by more recent arrivals building on the foundations of others.

As we learn to see an area through the eyes of the Lord, and seek His interpretation as to the reasons behind present-day issues affecting that place negatively, we also learn to see that such issues and problems may be based on the influence of earlier activities and the practices of previous tenants.

In *The Twilight Labyrinth* George Otis Jr. addresses the question "Why does spiritual darkness linger where it does?" His book gives many indications how the stewardship and activities of people both past and present open the door to spiritual evil on the land. Otis puts it this way:

> Careful readers will discover these clues [to spiritual darkness] in the form of heights, imaginations, gateways, rebellions, traumas, pacts, traditions, festivals and technology. Each of these signal themes comes with its own steamer trunk of revelations, and those patient enough to unpack them in proper order will find their way.[13]

We have observed that God is the Lord of history and geography, and that every nation in existence has been formed under His sovereignty. It is the same for every community, every church and every individual. Each has differing foundational principles, causing it to be not only distinct in personality and characteristics, but unique.

The Concise Oxford Dictionary defines *foundation* as "the solid ground or base, natural or artificial, on which a building rests," or "the basis, groundwork or underlying principle." Hebrews 11:10 refers to Abraham "looking forward to the city with foundations, whose architect and builder is God." Beckett writes:

> The Greek word for *foundations* in this passage means "rudimentary principles and precepts." Abraham was looking for a city whose foundations—rudimentary principles and precepts—were based on godly principles.[14]

The same word for *foundation* is used in 1 Corinthians 3:10, where Paul refers to the foundation of the human personality. In other words, every living entity made up of people is built on rudimentary principles and precepts. Cities are influenced in their development by people of the past who were part of the original vision-casting, formation and development of the city. Cities are also influenced by people of the present building on others' foundations.

We find the principle of foundational stewardship elsewhere in Scripture, including Isaiah 28:16: "See, I lay a stone in Zion, a tested stone, a precious cornerstone for a sure *foundation*; the one who trusts will never be dismayed" (emphasis added). In Ephesians 2:19–20 we are told that the citizens of God's household are "built on the foundation of the apostles and prophets, with Christ Jesus himself as the chief cornerstone." 2 Timothy 2:19 makes reference to "God's solid foundation" that "stands firm."

Foundations and Cities

In his impressive book *Taking Our Cities for God*, John Dawson states:

> I believe God intends the city to be a place of shelter, a place of communion and a place of personal liberation as its citizens practice a division of labor according to their own unique gifts. I believe our cities have the mark of God's sovereign purpose on them. Our cities contain what I call a redemptive gift.[15]

In traveling to many places around the globe, I have never found two cities with the same personality. Each city, like each nation and each person, has both negatives and positives. God longs to remove the fallen stewardship so as to release the fullness of His original vision and purpose in the life of each city (or nation or person).

During my first visit to New Orleans, I was amazed at the immorality and party-going spirit I experienced. Later, after reflection and research, I realized that God had intended this to be a city of celebration and hospitality, giving praise to His goodness and love.

In 1998, during a visit to Kiev in the Ukraine, I witnessed a city still affected by the Communist mindset and in which corruption and immorality were rampant. Yet in speaking with those wonderful Ukrainian people, I could sense extraordinary gifts of generosity and hospitality that they can offer to the rest of the world.

Ukrainians have suffered much and find it difficult to rejoice, in case their hopes are dashed. During World War II the Nazis took trainloads of dirt from this fertile nation that, according to some estimates, has a reservoir of rich topsoil twelve feet in depth. It could be a garden nation for the rest of the world. But the fallen stewardship of leaders like Hitler and Stalin and several others still affects the people in that part of the world. The Ukraine is a nation waiting to be released into its destiny as originally determined by God.

Every city becomes the receptacle of what is good and bad, depending on what people have done in that city. Those people are the stewards or influencers determining the foundations on which future generations of people live and build. Leaders in today's Church like John Dawson and Cindy Jacobs believe that cities have unique characteristics that can reflect the character and nature of God in that particular area. Indeed, fallen stewardship in a city can be cleansed and removed, so that transformation can take place. In Acts 8:4–8 we are told of an unnamed city in Samaria that was under the influence of the occult but that became a place of great joy after Philip ministered there.

God has a determined love for cities. We see this (among other places) in His conversation with Jonah over the destiny of Nineveh (Jonah 4:11). Likely, if enough faithful believers had been found, God would have saved Sodom and Gomorrah. We find Jesus weeping over Jerusalem (Luke 19:41) and giving significant detail to John concerning seven churches (Revelation 2–3). God knew the issues that had to be dealt with in those churches, and the distinct giftings He had prepared for each place.

Since the majority of people in the world live in cities, cities play a strategic role in the liberation and evangelization of people. As Robert Linthicum reminds us in *City of God, City of Satan*:

> It comes as a surprise to all of us; the Bible actually is an urban book! . . . The world of Moses and David and Daniel and Jesus was an urban world. . . . Their world was probably more urban than any civilization before it or any after it for the next fifteen hundred years.[16]

Linthicum goes on to point out, in this biblical theology of the urban church, that the Bible was written in a world dominated by cities. Indeed, he states that "Rome in the apostle Paul's day numbered more than one million people—the first city in history to exceed that number."[17] Cities, Linthicum believes, are crucial to God's overall strategy in redeeming His people; and while the whole world is a battlefield between good and evil, the greatest battles are taking place inside the city. Linthicum puts it this way:

> Every city has both Babylon and Jerusalem in it, for every city is the battleground between the god of Babylon (Baal, Satan) and the God of Jerusalem (Yahweh, The Lord) for dominion and control.[18]

The City—A Place of Mission and Transformation

Bear in mind that the battle over a city between God and Satan is not a battle between two equals. God can use the sin of a city for His higher purposes, and He alone has ultimate jurisdiction over the destiny of a city or nation. The degree to which God's presence and purpose are released in a city, however, may depend on the willingness of His servants in that city to obey His counsel and direction. It is our personal and corporate stewardship that gives access to Satan, or that opens up the hearts and lives of people to God.

Psalm 46 reminds us that God's presence safeguards and sanctifies the city of Jerusalem even in the midst of chaos and violence. If this is a reflection of what God wants for every urban setting, then the city, according to the psalmist, is God's primary dwelling place, and also the place that He sanctifies and blesses. Again, if Jerusalem is any reflection, Psalm 87:2 makes it clear that God loves the city. We learn from the examples of Nineveh and Sodom that He wants to save entire cities. Scripture reveals that the life of Jesus was developed in cities. In the early Church, apostles like Paul targeted cities as part of their mission strategy. In any city in which God dwells and His people become transformed, distress and violence are removed, and the economy grows and develops (see Psalm 144:14).

God longs to protect the city against all harm because of His love for that place. "There is a river whose streams make glad the city of God, the holy place where the Most High dwells. God is within her, she will not fall; God will help her at break of day" (Psalm 46:4–5). Similar to what we read in Psalm 144, Psalm 48:8 also suggests the sense of security that God gives to the city in which He dwells: "As we have heard, so have we seen in the city of the LORD Almighty, in the city of our God: God makes her secure forever." Psalm 48 ends with a thrilling statement concerning God's authority within a city: "This God is our God for ever and ever; He will be our guide even to the end."

The responsibility of the Church in every generation is to declare the Lord's presence in His city and in the midst of His people. This is where the majority of people unreached for Christ are to be found. But where sin exists and persists, people's eyes are blinded and their hearts hardened to the call of the Gospel. We must now go further in examining God's perspective concerning our stewardship of the land, since it affects our lives, our churches, our places of work, our communities, our cities and even our nations.

Part 2

THE STEWARDSHIP
OF LAND

THREE

SEEING AND BELIEVING: OUR WORLDVIEW AND PERSPECTIVE ON LAND

n order to appreciate the issues of stewardship and land from God's perspective, and to accept that there are consequences attached to this stewardship, we must first understand the importance of our worldview—the filter through which we interpret reality. Simply put, can we see things in the same way God does, since this has much bearing on our being able to see the issues of land through His eyes?

So far we have acknowledged our extraordinary responsibility, both individual and corporate, on behalf of God. He has entrusted to us the care of this world because the earth truly belongs to Him. We have also seen the seriousness of sin, both personal and corporate, whether active in a present generation or inherited from previous generations. (We will look at this issue in greater depth in the next chapter.)

All of this challenges our normal, day-to-day thinking and living! Consequently, how we view and accept the relationship between sin and fallen stewardship challenges us to reexamine the worldview through which we judge and interpret spiritual issues. Do we need to see things first and then believe, or can we believe first and then see? How veiled is our eyesight?

Let's consider the vision Paul had for his ministry. Recall from Acts 26:17–18 the four key ingredients in the commission he received from Jesus:

1. To open the eyes of the people.
2. To turn them from darkness to light.
3. To turn them from the power of Satan to God.
4. To ensure that they received forgiveness and sanctification by faith in Christ.

These four spiritual issues—necessary prerequisites to effective evangelism—require us to think *spiritually*. Ephesians 6 reminds us that we are dealing not with flesh and blood but with powers and principalities. Paul recognized that people had to be liberated from the power of sin, since the whole of their lives and work came under its influence. Once they were freed spiritually, then the rest of their stewardship could be addressed.

Contours of Religious Philosophy

In examining the worldview of most people in the West, I have found that, for the most part, our present mindset falls under this outline, which explains the contours of religious philosophy influencing us today:

Deism: God is around but not active.

Humanism: Man can do anything on his own, without God.

Secularism: God is irrelevant to individuals and society.

Religious pluralism: Everyone's belief system is equally acceptable.

Universalism: All will somehow be saved.

Most of us who are Christians would regard ourselves as *theists*, which according to Alan Richardson's *Dictionary of Christian Theology* means believing "in a single supreme being who is the source of everything else and who, ... being himself complete and perfect, is worthy to be worshipped."[1]

We say we believe in a living, active God who relates in our lives personally every day. In reality, however, many of us do not. The majority of the Western Church falls under the umbrella of *deism*. Again, quoting Richardson: "The deists [of the eighteenth century] held that reason itself was capable of demonstrating the propriety of believing in God as 'the Intelligent Author of Nature', and 'the Moral Governor of the World'. There is no need of any divine revelation."[2]

Rudy and Marny Pohl put it this way:

> Deism claims that God, after having created the world, wound it up like a clock, stepped back from it, and adopted a *laissez faire* or hands-off approach towards nations and history. This view sees nations as merely the creation of men and political processes, and sees history as essentially a random series of cause and effect events. It claims that God stands outside the world and does not involve Himself or intervene in the life and affairs of the nations, but rather, He expects humans to rationally and morally work things out between themselves.[3]

If God does not intervene intimately in the lives of His people or nations, there is little point in seeking His counsel and direction, and people are responsible for determining their own destinies with no significant reference to God.

Thus, in any nation under the influence of deism, there is little fear of God. Indeed in North America we have seen references to God eliminated in many public platforms—politically, morally and educationally. In the worldview of many of us, the cosmic personalities or forces in the top tier of religion relate little to the rest of our world, so that we go to work, to earn the money, to buy the bread, to get the strength, to go to work ...!

The worldview informed by Scripture, by contrast, teaches that God does, in fact, interrelate with us in everyday life. Paul the apostle was painfully aware of the reality of spiritual issues around him every day. But the intimacy between us and the cosmic realm today has been all but neutralized, due to the influence of deism in our thinking and spiritual practice.

Unless we have a healthy fear of God and are intimately acquainted with His intervention in our lives, both individual and corporate, then the spiritual part of our beings can lead us into the deceiving web of the occult and the subtlety of *pantheism*. The latter identifies the divine with all of reality, destroying the distinction between Creator and creation and leading us toward the subtle worship of creation rather than the Creator, which in turn becomes an open door for defilement on the land. (More on this in the next section.) Pantheism stands in direct contrast to theism, as does *atheism*, which denies the existence of God, and *agnosticism*, which regards the question of divine existence as unanswerable. As God's stewards we must make sure our spiritual antennae are fine-tuned to His perception of life and reality.

Unless our worldview is biblically based, we can eventually arrive at that final mindset on our list and fall under the influence of *universalism*, which some in the Church today endorse wholeheartedly. Universalism has reappeared as a present-day heresy, suggesting that God is such a great God of love that everyone will ultimately be saved according to his or her own belief system.

I heard teaching at a pastors' seminar on this subject, following which one of the pastors told me tearfully he was being sued by his denominational headquarters for preaching to his congregation that Jesus was God's only way to salvation. If he would recant and state that Jesus was but one of various routes to God, thus keeping in line with the political correctness of the day, then he would have his ordination papers returned. Such is the opinion of increasing numbers in our Western seminaries today! If we endorse universalism in its variety of subtleties, then sin and accountability for our actions become relative and subjective, and our management of the earth as God's stewards becomes inconsequential.

Our worldview does have an effect on how we live and what we do on the land. Only by rejecting such contours of religious philosophy and allowing a biblical worldview to govern our thinking and understanding will we learn from Scripture that our stewardship can have an extraordinary, positive cause and effect upon and within the world around us (as we will see in chapter 9).

We now need to go further with this line of reasoning and see the impact that our activities can and do have on the land in a negative sense when, as His stewards, we maintain a worldview different from that of Scripture and open the door to sin, which is forever crouching at the door.

Four Causes of Defilement

Ezra 9:11 graphically captures the emotion of God's heart when He sees sin in the lives of His people and on His land:

> . . . "The land you are entering to possess is a land polluted by the corruption of its peoples. By their detestable practices they have filled it with their impurity from one end to the other."

God is referring to the land and its people, soon to be occupied by His own people, and He continues with these admonitions:

"Therefore, do not give your daughters in marriage to their sons or take their daughters for your sons. Do not seek a treaty of friendship with them at any time, that you may be strong and eat the good things of the land and leave it to your children as an everlasting inheritance."

verse 12

Scripture teaches us that there are at least four major categories of sin and defilement, the result of fallen stewardship. Let us examine these in some depth.

1. Idolatry

Idolatry is the most serious sin in the eyes of God. We commit it when we allow anyone or anything else to take priority in our lives over Him. It is always connected with worship and involves honoring a spirit form other than God.

In Exodus 20:3–4 God makes clear that we are to have no other gods before Him, and that we are not to make for ourselves "an idol in the form of anything in heaven above or on earth beneath or in the waters below" that could take up a position of prominence in our lives. In verse 5 He says He is "a jealous God," and that idolatrous worship can lead to the punishment of children for the sins of their fathers up to the third and fourth generations. As a covenantal God, He expects us to maintain and honor our covenantal relationship with Him. If we do, verse 6 promises His love shown "to a thousand generations of those who love [Him] and keep [His] commandments."

Jeremiah 3:6–10 is one of many passages in Scripture that reveal the sin of idolatry. In verse 9 we read that "Israel's immorality mattered so little to her, she defiled the land and committed adultery with stone and wood." Here we are told that land is defiled due to idolatrous worship—when the worship of objects replaces the worship of God. Jeremiah 16:18 provides similar insight:

> "I will repay them double for their wickedness and their sin, because they have defiled my land with the lifeless forms of their vile images and have filled my inheritance with their detestable idols."

Idolatry also takes place when we worship the creation and ourselves more than our Creator (see Romans 1:24–25). Worshiping creation, coming under the influence of the occult, even unwittingly endorsing pantheism—these Western sins are also the practices of many nations found in the 10/40 Window, the area between the tenth and fortieth latitudes in which the vast majority of the world's unreached peoples live. Some missiologists calculate that Japan worships more than forty thousand idols; Nepal, as many as one million; India, more than three hundred million.

The influence of deism can subtly lead even believers into a pantheistic relationship with creation, in which ecology and the care of trees and water become more important than a relationship with God. Idolatry can also be found in the worship of oneself, when through pride or arrogance we feel we are able to chart our own course without any recognition of God. A church is in danger of committing idolatry when it excludes itself from the Body of Christ and sets itself up in an autonomous position over other church fellowships in any given area.

2. Immorality and Fornication

Idolaters are often led into immoral lifestyles because they have no sense of accountability before a living God. Leviticus 18:1–23 gives extensive insight into the issue of sexual impropriety. God makes clear in verses 24–25 that we are not to participate in this kind of lifestyle:

> Do not defile yourselves in any of these ways, because this is how the nations that I am going to drive out before you became defiled. Even the land was defiled; so I punished it for its sin, and the land vomited out its inhabitants.

Leviticus 18:22 and Romans 1:24–25 give clear insight as to the sin of homosexuality, in spite of the present-day rationalization in the Church at large. We have already seen that Leviticus 19:29 refers to prostitution turning the land into a place of wickedness, while Ezekiel 16:25–27 states:

> At the head of every street you built your lofty shrines and degraded your beauty, offering your body with increasing promiscuity to anyone who passed by. You engaged in prostitution with the Egyptians, your lustful neighbors, and provoked me to anger with your increasing promiscuity. So I stretched out my hand against you and *reduced your territory*; I gave you over to the greed of your enemies, the daughters of the Philistines, who were shocked by your lewd conduct.
>
> emphasis added

Notice again that our territory of influence and authority as God's people are reduced when we do not address prostitution in a forthright manner. This affects every level of society—educational, recreational, political, economic. It also affects the role of the family, the nuclear unit of society, and can cause a breakup of that vital unit. When the Church does not address immorality and fornication, she loses her "authority" in that location.

I recall visiting a city on the eastern coast of Canada and being driven past an influential church that I was told presented evangelical preaching yet affirmed a sexual lifestyle contrary to Scripture. It is the only time I ever recall being propositioned outside a church by two prostitutes working as a pair (never mind being propositioned by one!). The church had no impact whatsoever for positive change, I was told, in the community. Judging from my brief encounter, I could see why!

When immorality and fornication are not addressed, this can also increase the individual's personal lust for power and authority even by living in such a community, and thereby undermining the servant-spirit of humility so needed in our society. We are told that Jesus' picking up the towel in John 13 revealed the full extent of His love. In that act we see righteous, pure, selfless love, in contrast to the immoral love that defiles and controls people, churches, communities, cities and even nations. Lust for power and authority can also be seen in the political corruption of many nations. In the Ukraine and Russia, for example, organized crime has sown corruption in many levels of society, which has had a continual negative effect on the land.

When I visited Russia in June 1998, an Every Home for Christ regional director told me that the city of Moscow alone saw two million abortions in 1997—extremely high for a city of nine million. My EHC host in Kiev in the Ukraine discussed the great amount of immorality in that city and land; many women have several abortions in their lifetimes. This major area of defilement contributes to the impurity of the body in other ways, too, such as through drugs and alcohol, because of the need to gratify and fulfill oneself.

Little wonder Paul continued to remind the people of what their lifestyle in Christ should include and exclude (see Galatians 5:16–26; Colossians 3:5–10). He recognized the subtlety of living in a fallen world and our propensity to revert to sinful ways of living.

3. Bloodshed

Here is another major reason for defilement of the land that quickly leads to a breach in our covenant relationship with God. His command in Numbers 35:33–34 is clear:

61

"Do not pollute the land where you are. Bloodshed pollutes the land, and atonement cannot be made for the land on which blood has been shed, except by the blood of the one who shed it. Do not defile the land where you live and where I dwell, for I, the LORD, dwell among the Israelites."

Isaiah 59:2–3 puts it this way:

Your iniquities have separated you from your God; your sins have hidden his face from you, so that he will not hear. For your hands are stained with blood, your fingers with guilt. Your lips have spoken lies, and your tongue mutters wicked things.

Bloodshed includes the taking of innocent life and the untimely slaughter of suppressed people groups. Bloodshed of any type, from the past or in the present, affects us in a variety of ways, and often results in the nursing of criticism, anger, jealousy, bitterness and rage over succeeding generations.

Over the years I have often sensed anger or rage in a particular congregation, only to find out later that the church was built on a former site of aboriginal bloodshed. In one church where a team and I were ministering, our research revealed that the sanctuary had been constructed on a former pagan site used for idolatrous sacrifice. This had continued to fuel anger and rage in the community, we realized, as well as confusion regarding spiritual issues. It was affecting every part of church life—worship, evangelism, finances, youth work and all levels of relationships. Once the issue was prayed through, a different atmosphere permeated the entire church fellowship.

4. Broken Covenants

Isaiah 24:5–6 states that "the earth is defiled by its people; they have disobeyed the laws, violated the statutes and broken the everlasting covenant. Therefore a curse consumes the earth; its people must bear their guilt." We have already noted that ours is a covenantal God who has entered into relationship with His people.

The word *covenant* is one of the most important words in the entire Bible, if not *the* most important. When people entered into covenants with each other in Old Testament days—as in the case of David and Jonathan, for example (see 1 Samuel 18:3–4)—it was on an equals basis with an exchange of love, friendship and protection, usually ratified with the sharing of a meal, the slaying of an animal and the exchange of a weapon and even a belt. In the case of God and His people, He makes the covenant with us, and if we choose to submit to His conditions and come under His sovereign love and protection, then we receive all the blessings listed in Deuteronomy 28. If we reject the conditions, we receive the curses mentioned in the same chapter. Exodus 24 records the unanimous response of God's people, placing them under solemn responsibility to keep His conditions.

In the New Testament God renews His covenant with the human race through Jesus Christ, and, as with all covenants, seals it in blood (see Matthew 26:28). He places the covenant responsibility for His people on the Church, to which we need to say, "Amen." Let's recall the importance of Hebrews 10:28–29, in that we need to maintain the promises of this covenant if we are to enjoy and inherit the blessings made available through Jesus Christ—which include the breaking of curses over our land and the restoration of all that God has wanted for His people. This is divine love at its best! We are entering into the covenant Jesus made with His Church. But when a person or the Church violates that covenant, we make ourselves vulnerable to the consequences of broken promises at personal, family, church, community, city and even national levels.

What are these consequences that become the fruit of a deadly root? They include broken marriages and fractured families. Only limited trust develops between people, along with a sense of competitiveness, since no one wants to be subservient to anyone else. As a result of broken promises, the land becomes defiled. We need to note that it is people's sin that causes this defilement, which in turn becomes a curse on the land, in turn affecting all who dwell on it, whether families, businesses, people groups or even nations. Jeremiah 23:10 says that "the land is full of adulterers; because of the curse the land lies parched and the pastures in the desert are withered." Graphic words!

Several years ago I participated in the founding of a mission and prayer ministry called Joshua Connection Canada. Since then we have often been involved in praying through the roots and strongholds that have negatively affected people and places in a variety of measures. On one such occasion our ministry team was asked to pray through a school that had faced occultic problems and sexual impropriety for many years, affecting both staff and students.

As we spent time praying through the school, our research told us that the school had been built on an original native Indian site, after European settlers came and offered blankets to the native people in exchange for access to their land. The blankets were deliberately infected with smallpox, however, and the native population subsequently died out—but not before they cursed the land, and any subsequent tenants who would live and work on that land, in reaction to the broken agreement that was destroying them.

In the years that followed, serious problems of an occultic and sexual nature affected the life of the school built on the site.

When full repentance and forgiveness was undertaken on behalf of both people groups involved, utilizing representatives of these groups, spiritual cleansing, along with prayers for the healing of the land, took place. The result of the broken covenant was finally removed. Almost immediately an immense change came into the school. Because forgiveness and reconciliation had transpired, the enemy no longer had access to that domain.

God, Man, Land and the Sabbath

We have already noted the intimate connection between God, man, land and the covenant. Now let's examine it in greater depth, recognizing why we need to maintain a biblical worldview at all times.

Defilement is a serious issue in the eyes of the Lord, especially when it is practiced by His own people. 1 Samuel 2:27–36 describes God's reaction to the sin of the priest Eli, who allowed unholiness and sin into the household of God. Eli's children also compromised the holiness of God, thus invoking His judgment. In Exodus 32 Aaron yielded to the wishes of the Israelites, who grew tired of waiting for Moses to come down from the mountain. Their sin of transgression and presumption filled the land, invoking God's wrath and resulting in a plague that struck the people.

Whenever mankind is filled with self, rather than with the Holy Spirit, the land and those who dwell on it suffer the consequences. Judges 21:25 refers to "every man [doing] that which was right in his own eyes" (KJV) in the absence of leadership. 2 Chronicles 15:3 refers to a time when the people of God were without a teaching priest, which meant the law was not taught, and as a result "turmoil" and "distress" came on people and nations (verses 5–6). In other words, the land and its inhabitants suffered the consequences of sin and unholy living, and the glory of the Lord would not rest on the people.

It is crucial, therefore, for us to understand God's teaching on this subject of man, land and sin.

Leviticus 26:14–39 refers to the punishment and judgment God must bring on His people when they continue to break the Torah and live lives of disobedience before Him. But we should note verses 34–35, which add an intriguing perspective to the relationship between God and man:

> "The land will enjoy its sabbath years all the time that it lies
> desolate and you are in the country of your enemies; then the

land will rest and enjoy its sabbaths. All the time that it lies desolate, the land will have the rest it did not have during the sabbaths you lived in it."

How exactly does the land enter into a time of rest? How can land enjoy its sabbath? Exodus 23:10–13 provides insight:

"For six years you are to sow your fields and harvest the crops, but during the seventh year let the land lie unplowed and unused. Then the poor among your people may get food from it, and the wild animals may eat what they leave. Do the same with your vineyard and your olive grove. Six days do your work, but on the seventh day do not work, so that your ox and your donkey may rest and the slave born in your household, and the alien as well, may be refreshed. Be careful to do everything I have said to you. . . ."

In keeping with the law, God expected His covenant to be extended to the land on which man worked and lived. The land was intended to enjoy a sabbath every seventh year. No work was to take place on it, during which time the poor could gather unharvested food and the animals enjoy some nourishment. When man did not give this seventh year of rest to the land, then both man and land suffered severe consequences.

Returning to Leviticus 26, verses 40–41 refer to the people confessing their sins and the sins of their fathers, to which God responds in verses 42–43:

"I will remember my covenant with Jacob and my covenant with Isaac and my covenant with Abraham, *and I will remember the land.* For the land will be deserted by them and will enjoy its sabbaths while it lies desolate without them . . ."

emphasis added

Much later Ezekiel 22 refers to priests, princes and prophets all misusing their stewardship of the land, and priests "[shutting] their eyes to the keeping of my Sabbaths, so that I am profaned among them" (Ezekiel 22:26). In verse 29: "The people of the land practice extortion and commit robbery; they oppress the poor and needy and mistreat the alien, denying them justice."

In the Hebrew way of thinking, standing before the Lord on behalf of the land (see verse 30) was fulfilling the role of legal representative, in order that God would not have to destroy the land due to the effects of the sin still resident in it.

It is clear from Scripture, then, that not giving the land its rest was a serious offense before God, because He is a covenantal God and the covenant on the land was to reveal His nature, character and love. Any unholiness practiced on the part of God's people on the land brought a grave breach in their relationship with Him.

The people broke this expectation of God's law. They practiced extortion and robbery and oppressed the poor by denying them access to the land during its sabbath, or seventh, year. Blatant usury took place, along with an extraordinary interpretation of keeping the Sabbath. At times the Israelites rented the land to the Gentiles, having them work the land, since they were not under the regulation of the Sabbath. Both parties split the profits. The Israelites were convinced they had not broken any part of the covenant—but God saw this from a very different perspective!

God's way of getting man's attention was to release judgment on His people, which is what He decreed in Deuteronomy 28. We need to examine this subject of God's judgment in greater detail.

Four Judgments of God on the Land

We have already discussed four major categories of sin and defilement: idolatry, immorality, bloodshed and broken covenants.

Each of these is the result of fallen stewardship. Whenever people sin on the land, the land suffers the consequences and reflects the judgments God sends on His people. Let's have a closer look at some of these consequences.

In his book *Healing the Land,* Winkie Pratney states:

> Famine, ecological devastation, war and disease are four prophetic voices designed to get our attention when our moral madness is full. What we do not want to acknowledge will not be overlooked—that we cannot get away with living as if God does not exist or as if He has nothing to say to us.[4]

There is no doubt about it. History proves again and again that when people ignore God, they often bring multiple tragedies on themselves. When people do not listen to God, or when they ignore His parameters of correct stewardship, they suffer the consequences of a curse that comes on that land. As Pratney points out:

> Israel was promised land by God for her future identity and inheritance so long as she was true to Him. If she remained faithful, she would not have to be sojourners forever like Abraham "looking for a country," wanderers like those who died in the "long, dusty desert" without entering the land of promise, exiles like those of the captivity in Babylon.[5]

When land is defiled through any of the categories we have just examined, certain results follow. Ezekiel 14 records the four main judgments of God that will visit an offending land.

1. Famine

> "Son of man, if a country sins against me by being unfaithful and I stretch out my hand against it to cut off its food supply and send famine upon it and kill its men and their animals. . . ."

> Ezekiel 14:13

All over the world we find vivid examples of famine in land where people have been disobedient before God. This includes the *physical hunger* experienced in any territory. Psalm 105:16 says: "He called down famine on the land and destroyed all their supplies of food."

It also includes famine of *the Word of God*. Amos 8:11 puts it this way:

> "The days are coming," declares the Sovereign LORD, "when I will send a famine through the land—not a famine of food or a thirst for water, but a famine of hearing the words of the LORD."

There is also a famine of *authenticity*—that is, a hunger for our real identity in Christ. Without this authenticity, we continue trying to "find ourselves" in other forms of idolatrous and self-fulfilling activity. We never really experience our primary purpose for life, or our giftings, or our identity made so clear in Christ.

We also experience a famine of *witness*. We hunger for a sense of God's presence in and through us—one we can share with other people. Yet there is an emptiness and void that only God can fill. It is as if His presence is absent from us, since the sin that permeates the land keeps His holiness from our midst.

There is also a famine in our *relationship to God as well as to other people*. The land is void of anything that reflects His nature and love. Spiritual sterility settles into the area. Relationships among people become anemic, without any real substance and depth.

Finally we experience a famine of *harvest*. This means there is little productivity in the lives of God's people. Fruitlessness replaces fruitfulness.

This type of famine leads us to examine the second warning God gives concerning fallen stewardship.

2. Ecological Devastation

"If I send wild beasts through that country and they leave it childless and it becomes desolate so that no one can pass through it because of the beasts, . . . the land would be desolate."

Ezekiel 14:15–16

A series of natural disasters is affecting the world in our time. While this has been the case in every generation, North America is undergoing earthquakes, hurricanes, floods, ice storms, drought and harvest failure to a point never before experienced.

Considering the amount of sowing taking place, the yields of our harvests are minimal at best. As I have monitored the prairies in Canada over the past several years, I have noted that each year sees either insect infestation, too much rain, sudden ice, too much sun, too much wind or other such problems, resulting in stunted harvests. This is taking place, interestingly enough, right in the area of a former Bible belt. One of the local farmers said to me not long ago, "Perhaps our problem is due to the fact that we have turned from God."

From a spiritual perspective, ecological devastation also involves little harvesting in the lives of people and little productivity as a whole. "The land lies parched" (Jeremiah 23:10) and "both prophet and priest are godless" (verse 11).

God seems to be reminding us through this kind of warning that He controls the natural elements required for a good harvest, both physically on the land and spiritually in our lives, and that little growth and productivity will take place if He is not honored and worshiped (see Jeremiah 3:1–4). Spiritual and physical harvest are always closely connected in Scripture. Amos 4:7 puts it this way:

> I also withheld rain from you when the harvest was still three months away. I sent rain on one town, but withheld it from another. One field had rain; another had none and dried up.

70

Haggai 1:9–11 reveals that God controls the full productivity of our labor. Here we have land with enormous potential and natural resources that yields very little in the hands of the people who are distanced from God:

> "You expected much, but see, it turned out to be little. What you brought home, I blew away. Why?" declares the LORD Almighty. "Because of my house, which remains a ruin, while each of you is busy with his own house. Therefore, because of you the heavens have withheld their dew and the earth its crops. I called for a drought on the fields and the mountains, on the grain, the new wine, the oil and whatever the ground produces, on men and cattle, and on the labor of your hands."

Concerning this Scripture, Pratney comments:

> It is no secret that the Western world faces a staggering economic burden. The causes are many, the warnings dire, the consequences frightening. Yet the root cause is none of the usual factors on which we usually lay blame. The root cause is *moral*. The source: personal selfishness, greed and carelessness.[6]

How true it is that if we sin against God, even nature turns against us! Each of us, from our respective nations, needs to examine the level at which stewardship defilement may have penetrated our lives, homes, churches, cities and nations. Let's ask God tenaciously to reveal to us if any of the problems we experience every day is because the land is defiled and awaits redemption.

In His grace, especially when people forget Him, God allows tragedies to come our way in order to sober us up so we can see things from His perspective.

3. War

> "Or if I bring a sword against that country and say, 'Let the sword pass throughout the land,' and I kill its men and their animals. . . ."
>
> Ezekiel 14:17

We assume that war involves the assault of one nation against another. This kind of sword, however, includes anger, jealousy, resentment, competitiveness, aloofness and divisiveness. All these reflect the opposite of what Jesus wants for His people, instead revealing the war within us that can take place at any level of society. This includes battles in the Church over sound or faulty doctrine; warfare in our homes; fighting between members of a household; and conflicts in outside relationships. It covers conflicts at work and issues between employers and employees and trade unions. And it includes warfare at the government level and all the petty striving that is given so much media attention.

These are the judgments that come on people when the land is defiled and that defilement is not properly addressed.

4. Disease

God speaks to His prophet with these words:

> "Or if I send a plague into that land and pour out my wrath upon it through bloodshed, killing its men and their animals, as surely as I live, declares the Sovereign LORD, even if Noah, Daniel and Job were in it, they could save neither son nor daughter. They would save only themselves by their righteousness."
>
> Ezekiel 14:19–20

Believers today are finding that when the tools of spiritual mapping and intercessory prayer are used correctly and applied to a community or city or nation suffering from disease, we can often trace the history of that disease to an actual time of defilement in which the sin of the people gave the enemy legal access to that area, as implied in Ephesians 4:27–28.

The medical analogy in all this is fairly evident. If a disease is present, we must find the source and destroy it at that point, or else discover the correct antidote. (We call this epidemiological investigation, based on the science and study of epidemics.) When cholera broke out in London in the 1840s, it was essential to find the initial cause (a water tap) in order to stem the problem. In a 1995 film entitled *Outbreak*, starring Dustin Hoffman, a disease was spreading rapidly in North America and elsewhere, all because of a monkey smuggled illegally out of its home environment. After it had bitten the first person and injected a deadly disease, an epidemic was now at hand, and the race was on to find the monkey. It was the source of the deadly disease, and *with the source came the solution!*

Disease itself brings a variety of fruit with it—anxieties, sorrow (see Psalm 103) and all forms of illness—physical, emotional, mental, spiritual.

God is saying again and again, "Don't ignore Me!" We must remember that "the earth is the LORD's and everything in it, the world, and all who live in it" (Psalm 24:1). The world needs to relinquish its self-confidence and sense of its own importance and acknowledge once again the supremacy of the sovereign God. As with physical disease, we need to discover the source of spiritual disease, since when we discover the cause, the solution lies close at hand.

These Judgments Lie Ahead

These four judgments we have reviewed from Ezekiel also face the last generation of mankind:

> I looked, and there before me was a pale horse! Its rider was named Death, and Hades was following close behind him. They were given power over a fourth of the earth to kill by sword, famine and plague, and by the wild beasts of the earth.
>
> Revelation 6:8

Here the New Testament is validating the warnings of the Old. If we understand God's perspective on land, we will also understand His perspective on mankind. As Winkie Pratney puts it:

> Touch the land and you touch mankind. Not until the land itself begins to fail do people begin to realize that something is badly wrong.[7]

God's Worldview on Sin

It is essential, as we have seen, that we hold a worldview that sees sin from God's perspective, if we are to try to understand and address it from His point of view.

A Christian worldview, as we have already seen, is one that understands the nature and existence of the spiritual realm around us, and how this spiritual realm influences us as people, both negatively and positively. While we are not addressing spiritual warfare in this book per se, the reality of spiritual warfare nevertheless lies behind the theme.

In *The Believer's Guide to Spiritual Warfare*, Tom White considers spiritual warfare at various levels. He sees a "prehistoric and ongoing conflict between the Creator and His faithful angels on the one side, and the rebellious hierarchy of evil forces under Satan on the other."[8] White sees the second level as the battle between the demonic realm and the redeemed, with Jesus giving His authority to the believers to encounter the enemy based on His victory on the cross. The third major level of spiritual warfare, according to White, is one in which deceived non-Christians are placed in various forms of bondage (Acts 26:18; 2 Corinthians 4:4; Ephesians 2:2).

White is clear that the Church is engaged in war over the lives of people at all levels, and he explains this through his understanding of the organized hierarchy of rulers or principalities *(archai)*, authorities *(exousia)*, powers *(dunamis)* and spiritual forces of evil *(kosmokratoras)*. White sees the *archai* as high-level satanic princes set over the nations and regions of the earth, while the word *exousia* connotes both supernatural and natural government. *Dunamis* operate within countries and cultures to influence certain aspects of life, while *kosmokratoras* are the various types of evil spirits that commonly afflict people.[9]

Probably the most comprehensive biblical description indicating a hierarchy in the demonic realm is that found in Ephesians 6:12:

> Our struggle is not against flesh and blood, but against the rulers, against the authorities, against the powers of this dark world and against the spiritual forces of evil in the heavenly realms.

Paul uses four distinct terms to describe the infrastructure of this demonic realm—terms that are the subject of much contemporary theological reflection. The word *archas* is generally translated "rulers" or "principalities," the word *exousias* as "authorities," the word *kosmokratoras* as "world rulers" and the term *pneumatika tes ponerias in tois epouraniois* as "the spiritual forces of evil in the heavenly realms." It is plain from this passage that these are the forces with which the Church wrestles and must overcome.

Rulers and Authorities

One of the most profound Scriptures in the New Testament describing the function of the Church is Ephesians 3:10:

> His intent was that now, through the church, the manifold wisdom of God should be made known to the *rulers* and *authorities* in the heavenly realms. . . .

emphasis added

Here the two words *archai* and *exousias* are used to describe the purpose of the Church—that is, to make known "the manifold wisdom of God" to all "rulers and authorities in the heavenly realms." The implication is that these rulers and authorities rule spiritually in the heavenly realms.

The same two words are found in Colossians 2:15:

> Having disarmed the powers and authorities, [Christ] made a public spectacle of them, triumphing over them by the cross.

The word *archai* is also found in Romans 8:38, which the New International Version translates as "demons."

The use of the words *archas* and *exousias* implies that these two demonic entities rule with significant authority in the demonic realm.

Both words are also used, however, in Ephesians 1:21, describing Christ's exalted reign in the heavenlies, "far above all *rule* and *authority,* power and dominion, and every title that can be given, not only in the present age but also in the one to come" (emphasis added). In other words, Christ's *archas* and *exousias* (as well as His *dunamis*) indicate His sovereignty over all other rulers and authorities and powers, whether earthly or heavenly. Paul emphasizes this point at the end of the verse when he indicates that this status of Christ is both for the present age and the age to come.

Further evidence of Paul's thinking in this area is found in Colossians 1:16:

> By him all things were created: things in heaven and on earth, visible and invisible, whether thrones or powers or rulers (*archai*) or authorities (*exousias*); all things were created by him and for him.

This is similar to Colossians 2:10, indicating Christ as "the head over every rule and authority," whether earthly or heavenly.

World Rulers

In his *Handbook for Spiritual Warfare* Dr. Ed Murphy writes about the next category of demonic entities described in Ephesians 6:12:

> The apostle follows *rulers* and *powers* with a phrase that is not used anywhere else in the New Testament or in the LXX: *tous kosmokratoras tou skotous toutou,* "the world rulers of this darkness."[10]

Concerning this same phrase, Clinton Arnold, in his book *Ephesians' Power and Magic,* writes:

> The source of this term has baffled interpreters since it does not appear in Jewish writings until the Testament of Solomon and since there is no use of the term in any extant pre-Christian literature or inscriptions. This evidence suggests that the term was current in both the magical tradition and astrology when the author wrote this epistle.[11]

Arnold further adds that the term was used "as one of a number of descriptive titles for various gods/spirits called on to aid the conjurer [on how to conjure up a god]."[12]

The use of this term certainly indicates demonic activity of some significant nature, but Tom White suggests that such activity would come from the lower end of the demonic infrastructure, being "the evil powers confronted and cast out in most deliverance sessions,"[13] such as spirits of deception, divination, lust, rebellion, fear and infirmity.

Spiritual Forces of Evil

Here is how Clinton Arnold describes the final phrase in Ephesians 6:12, *pneumatika tes ponerias in tois epouranios:*

> The writer finishes this list of powers not with a new category, but with a comprehensive designation for all the classes

of hostile spirits. . . . Believers need to be prepared to engage all the forces of evil in battle.[14]

We can conclude that Paul is using a combination of words and phrases in order to describe evil spiritual forces that exist in some form of infrastructure within the demonic realm. Clearly, as Ed Murphy puts it,

> Our battle against the Devil is *not* with him personally or individually. It is with him only as he operates against us *through* evil, high-level cosmic principalities and powers.[15]

The implication is that this infrastructure of demonic powers can have a significant effect on our lives at any level of society, including both "kingdoms" (notions of human power) and the systems and structures found in the *kosmos*.

In this sentiment Walter Wink, in *Naming the Powers: The Language of Power in the New Testament,* says that *archai* and *exousias* refer not only to personal spiritual forces, but also to a social-cultural-institutional view of spiritual evil. In other words, the world's institutions, laws, traditions and even rituals are to be included under these spiritual forces. We will see shortly why this is important for us to understand, in that the entire sociopolitical infrastructure of a community can be under demonic influence based on an original and continuing defilement of the land. Wink also believes that the word *kosmokratoras* can include all forms of institutional idolatry.[16]

The point is, Christians need to be aware of the supernatural powers that exist *behind* institutions, more than simply the human agents that so often represent them. The infrastructure of all the human systems in the world is subject to the influence of these spiritual powers. This would explain the first part of Paul's thinking in Ephesians 6:12—"Our struggle is not against flesh and blood"—and his directive in the following verses for us to appropriate the armor of God that is part of our spiritual equipping in our struggle against Satan and his evil forces.

As we have seen, there is both controversy and diversity over the specific meaning and application of the New Testament words describing the nature and influence of Satan's evil forces. For our purposes, we need to realize simply that these evil forces have varying levels of power and authority to the degree that they are given access to people and society.

How Does Sin Gain a Foothold?

How do these spiritual entities or forces gain access to our lives, whether individually or corporately? The simplest answer is, *Through the action of sin, whether past or present, whether individual or corporate.* We need to examine this further in order to understand the issue of stewardship and sin, and the witting or unwitting permission we give the demonic realm in gaining access to our lives.

Part of the answer lies in the explanation of Ephesians 4:27: "Do not give the devil a foothold." The Greek word as used here for "foothold" is *topon*, which comes from *topos*, a root word meaning "a place or locality or piece of land." *Topos* is also the root for our English word *topographical*, a cartographic term representing the surface features of a place or region.

Paul's use of the word *topos* in this verse is fascinating. He purposely uses a geographical term indicating the right of occupancy. If we sin at the *kosmokratoras* level, to use Tom White's perspective on these terms, and do not deal with the effects of that sin, then our area of influence where we live becomes subject to the legal access of the demonic realm. C. Peter Wagner in his book *Warfare Prayer* describes it this way:

> A person who is demonized is not per se a demonic person, but rather a victim of a powerful demonic force. Likewise,

social structures are not, in themselves, demonic, but they can be and often are demonized by some extremely pernicious and dominating demonic personalities, which I call territorial spirits.

The view I am advocating at least permits a theology of hope. It opens up the possibility that social structures, like demonized human beings, can be delivered from demonic oppression through warfare prayer. This is why I believe that history belongs to the intercessors.[17]

Sin, whether on the part of an individual, a group of people, a city or a nation, gives a legal foothold to the enemy. He is able to feed on that sin, thereby gaining right of access to that area where the holiness of God is not being honored or observed. The demonic infrastructure reinforces itself over time, and as sin permeates the area, the foothold of the demonic extends and embeds itself.

Sin—whether personal or generational or corporate; whether based on occult involvement or invited through membership in an organization with occultic roots (like Freemasonry) or transferred into a community through the cultural vehicle of people groups—provides the enemy with the right of access to an area. Once again, it comes through the influence of our stewardship.

Kosmos *and Kingdoms*

When Paul refers to "the ruler of the kingdom of the air" (Ephesians 2:2), he uses the Greek word *kosmos*, the same word Jesus uses in John 14:30, referring to "the prince of this world." *Kosmos* means "human systems and governments." When sin is not dealt with, the enemy has the right of legal access to whatever part of the *kosmos* is defiled by that fallen stewardship.

In Matthew 4:8–9 the devil tempts Jesus in the wilderness by showing Him the kingdoms of the world in their glory. Here the Greek word for *kingdoms* is *basileia*, implying ruling and controlling. Satan was offering Jesus the right to rule over human systems and governments, but from Satan's perspective.

Basileia and the *kosmos* are subject to Satan's legal access, or any part of his demonic infrastructure, as long as topical defilement goes unaddressed. This principle is true for a person, a building or an area of land.

It explains the missionary dilemma referred to in the last chapter, in which one part of a community is difficult to evangelize while another part responds. This is because the *topos* of the first area is subject to the defilement of sin, and the eyes and hearts of the people are unable to hear or receive the Gospel of Christ. When they go to the other side of the community, however, the demonic does not have the same degree of access or influence, and the spiritual climate is quite different.

When the people of God repent of the sin that has taken place in any given area, both originally and over the years, and any known bondages are broken, and any resident spirits removed, and healing is declared over the land and its people, then God's presence can once again permeate that area. We will see more of this process (it is often called identificational repentance) in chapter 7.

The Effects of Sin

When we consider sin, on both an individual and corporate basis, certain factors emerge.

First, sin almost always results in *feelings of guilt and shame*, as we see in Genesis 3 after the fall of Adam and Eve. Sin makes us want to hide from God. Because we do not want to face the truth about an issue, we tend to justify and rationalize our sinfulness before God and others.

Sin also causes *reactionary sin in others' lives*. Moral cowardice causes us to blame others. We see this again in Genesis 3 when Adam blames Eve for his sin. We become more conscious of self and self-preservation. Sin causes us to be suspicious of other

81

people, and it releases anger and hate. This is easily seen at the level of the local church when sin has not been dealt with in a given situation (for example, in finances, choir, fellowship groups, evangelism or outreach). It is in these areas of church involvement where relationships are almost always strained and fragile.

Sin brings *fear and mistrust* into our lives. We no longer want to open up to other people.

Romans 6:23 states categorically that "the wages of sin is death." Sin evokes *God's judgment from the cross.*

And, as we have already seen, sin gives the enemy *a foothold* in any given situation.

Sin that is not dealt with also releases the "accuser of our brothers, who accuses them before our God day and night" (Revelation 12:10). The accuser of the brethren accuses only twice, according to this passage: *day and night!* This makes a person or community vulnerable to both *demonic activity and accusation,* as long as that sin is permitted to remain. (It may, however, appear in a variety of wardrobe outfits over the years!)

What we have seen so far is based on a healthy biblical world-view. How God views sin, defilement, judgment and spiritual issues is essential for our understanding if we are to address all these issues effectively, as they influence people and land. We must not forget that we are called to be His stewards, and that these issues are also our issues. When the effect of individual and corporate sin is not addressed, it becomes fodder for *bondages and strongholds.*

It is to this aspect of fallen stewardship that we now turn, and how strongholds can affect people and nations—even generationally.

FOUR

~

STRONGHOLDS
AND STEWARDSHIP

In order to deal with strongholds effectively, we need to know first how to identify them. *New Webster's Dictionary and Thesaurus* defines a stronghold as "a fortress; a center of support for a cause or faction."[1]

In his book *That None Should Perish* Ed Silvoso defines a stronghold as "a mindset impregnated with hopelessness that causes us to accept as unchangeable situations that we know are contrary to the will of God."[2]

Cindy Jacobs, in *Possessing the Gates of the Enemy*, defines strongholds as "fortified places Satan builds to exalt himself against the knowledge and plans of God."[3] This brief but workable definition draws on the meaning of Paul's words in 2 Corinthians 10:4: "The weapons we fight with are not the weapons of the world. On the contrary, they have divine power to demolish strongholds."

In *Breaking Strongholds* Tom White says Jesus was continually dealing with strongholds of unbelief, doubt, self-will and rebellion. He defines a stronghold as "an entrenched pattern of thought, an ideology, value, or behavior that is contrary to the word and will of God."[4] White believes that strongholds exist within people that are traceable to, and exploited by, satanic forces. We need to utilize divine weapons in order to expose and tear down strongholds that are blatantly anti-Christian.

The index of a book edited by C. Peter Wagner, *Breaking Strongholds in Your City,* refers to all of the following: spiritual strongholds, strongholds between city and church, ideological strongholds, national strongholds, occultic strongholds, strongholds of iniquities, strongholds of the mind, strongholds of tradition, sectarian strongholds, social strongholds, territorial strongholds and trauma-induced strongholds.[5] These are the different means, or points of entry, through which Satan manages to infiltrate people, families, churches and cities. Through them different lifestyles or kinds of thinking are released contrary to the will of God for His people. Such is the diversity of spiritual warfare!

George Otis Jr., in his *Glossary of Related Terms with Regard to Spiritual Mapping and Spiritual Warfare,* defines spiritual strongholds as "ideological fortresses that exist both in the human mind and in objective territorial locations. Manifesting both offensive and defensive characteristics, these strongholds simultaneously will repel light and export darkness."[6] A publication edited by Otis with Mark Brockman, *Strongholds of the 10/40 Window,* points out that one can easily assume strongholds are idolatrous sites, or perhaps even demons themselves, although neither is true. Rather,

> Spiritual strongholds are invisible structures of thought and authority that are erected through the combined agency of demonic influence and human will. In this sense they are not demons, but the place from which demons operate.[7]

How do strongholds originate and how are they passed along? In *The Twilight Labyrinth* Otis offers this perspective:

First, strongholds are born whenever cultures welcome evil powers into their midst through unambiguous pacts; and second, strongholds are extended when the provisions of these pacts are honored by successive generations.[8]

Lying behind each culture is a spiritual influence such as what we find in Hinduism, Islam, Buddhism or Confucianism. Otis offers four possible explanations for how the spiritual powers behind each culture are sustained from one generation to another:

1. Religious festivals and pilgrimages
2. Cultural traditions (especially initiation rites and ancestor worship)
3. Adaptive deceptions (or syncretism)
4. Unresolved social injustices[9]

Behind any one of these four explanations, Otis believes, lie "conscious transactions with the spirit world, occasions for successive generations to reaffirm choices and pacts made by their ancestors."[10]

As I have developed the theology of stewardship of the land over the last several years, I have formed my own working definition of a stronghold:

> A sphere of influence on and within our lives, families, churches, communities, cities and even nations that feeds on sin (both individual and corporate, personal and inherited) and that gives *spiritual and geographical leverage* to the enemy of God's people, thus blinding them to the truth of seeing things from God's perspective.

As we saw in the last chapter, in our study of worldview, the way a person *thinks* influences his or her personal stewardship, which in turn influences other people and places. This influence can originate from either an inherited or a geographical stronghold, which could, therefore, have a significant influence on people's response to the Gospel of Christ.

All the definitions we have looked at offer clarification of strongholds. Each infers that people are deceived, or at least influenced, in the way they think or in the way they evaluate things. But current studies, with their focus on spiritual warfare, tend to narrow our view of strongholds to solely negative connotations. This is not surprising when we realize that much of Scripture presents strongholds in a negative perspective. But this is not the whole scriptural picture. We must not lose sight of a stronghold as an important part of God's plan of protection for His people.

Before we observe how negative strongholds are given access to our lives, then, and how these can be released or transferred from person to person, let's look at strongholds from a different perspective.

The Biblical Setting for Strongholds

The *Interpreter's Dictionary of the Bible* says that the words *stronghold* and *fortress* are used alternately in Scripture.[11] In addition this Bible dictionary cross-references the word *stronghold* with the words *citadel, palace, defense, castle, fort* and *force.* In other words, a stronghold can be any one of these points of reference—a fortified city, a fortified place, a secure height or refuge, or a citadel—symbolic of God as a protection and refuge.[12]

The NIV translates Isaiah 33:16 this way: "This is the man who will dwell on the heights, whose *refuge* will be the mountain fortress. His bread will be supplied, and water will not fail him" (emphasis added). The Revised Standard Version says, "His place of defense will be the fortresses of rocks." The New King James Version identifies it as "the fortress of rocks."

These translations use three words—*refuge, defense* and *fortress*—all with the same meaning: a place of security and protection.

The Interpreter's Dictionary also defines the word *citadel* as "a stronghold of a city or palace for the purposes of defense or domination." It explains that David conquered Jerusalem by taking the fortress or citadel of the city (see 2 Samuel 5:7, 9; 1 Chronicles 11:5, 7). Here the Hebrew use of the word may refer to a fortified tower or building, and in addition to being defined as a "citadel," it is rendered variously as *tower* (Psalm 122:7, RSV); *fortress* (Amos 1:12); *stronghold* (Isaiah 34:13); *palace* (Jeremiah 6:5, RSV); and *castle* (Proverbs 18:19, KJV and RSV).[13]

Towers, a common feature of the biblical landscape, were located in cities, pastures, vineyards and farmlands. Towers were built of brick or stone and varied greatly in size, serving chiefly for refuge or defense against military attack. Some were small stone rooms serving as watchtowers in vineyards, as Mark 12:1 suggests. Some were large enough to serve as citadels or fortresses into which the population of the village could retreat at a time of danger (see Judges 9:51). Some towers were of such biblical significance that they were actually named in Scripture, such as the tower of David (see Song of Solomon 4:4).

The New Bible Dictionary refers to strongholds under two other classifications: fortification and siegecraft.[14] This dictionary indicates that the word *fortress* is related to the words *stronghold* and *fenced cities*. The rebuilding of Jerusalem under Nehemiah was a good example of the biblical understanding that walls make a city. Whenever possible a natural, defensible site was chosen for the location of a city. A steep, isolated peak with an impregnable spur of a hill was an excellent spot, especially if a stream was at hand. City walls would run as high as thirty feet to help ensure protection.[15]

It is interesting to note the variety of English words used to interpret Hebrew thought in this subject of strongholds. In the thinking of the ancient world, the word *stronghold* (or any of its synonymous terms) implied a sense of significant strength, protection and refuge. In other words, this type of "stronghold thinking," as a major point of reference in the life of the Bible, has to do with *defense*. The ancient world lived with the knowledge that unless their fortresses, strongholds or fenced cities were well secured, they could easily be plundered by a conquering people.

Strongholds and God's People

Before we go on to explore the negative, deceptive aspect of strongholds, let's note four underlying themes from Scripture:

1. God is our stronghold.
2. We lost our protection through the Fall.
3. God will destroy anything that sets itself up as a stronghold in our lives.
4. We are to demolish strongholds that set themselves up against God.

1. God Is Our Stronghold

The words *stronghold* and *fortress* always describe God as the refuge of the righteous: a fortified city, a fortified place, a secure height, a citadel. While the Bible uses these words in a literal sense, it is clear about their purpose in a figurative sense as well. Here are just a few (italics added to highlight the word in each case):

> The LORD is a refuge for the oppressed, a *stronghold* in times of trouble.
>
> Psalm 9:9

The LORD is my *rock*, my *fortress* and my *deliverer*; my God is my rock, in whom I take refuge. He is my shield and the horn of my salvation, my *stronghold*.

Psalm 18:2

O my Strength, I watch for you; you, O God, are my *fortress*, my loving God.

Psalm 59:9–10

The LORD is good, a *refuge* [KJV, *stronghold*] in times of trouble. He cares for those who trust in him.

Nahum 1:7

2. We Lost Our Protection through the Fall

The Bible is clear about God's desire to be our stronghold. It was that way from the beginning. In the Garden of Eden God was a stronghold for Adam and Eve. When their desire for sin resulted in the Fall, they left the safety of their stronghold. They would be openly vulnerable to the enemy's attack unless they returned to their Protector with repentance and humility.

This is the underlying theme of much of the Old Testament. When God was not the stronghold of His people, the enemy of their souls plundered them, subjecting them to negative strongholds that kept them in captivity. This applied to every facet of their living and thinking—ideological, political, cultural, spiritual and moral. *The type of stronghold that protects and secures people at any given time becomes the means by which these people live and are defined.*

But God did not give up. Throughout the Old Testament we have the sense in which He, speaking through the Psalms and prophets, refers to winning back what was lost—even though sometimes this meant His righteous anger bore down on His people until they saw the need for repentance.

3. God Will Destroy Other Strongholds

When God's people engaged in idolatrous worship, their defiling stewardship resulted in the removal of the stronghold of the Lord and the raising up of the stronghold of the new false deity instead. This is fallen stewardship, which incurred the wrath of God. Divine judgment sometimes resulted, as seen in Lamentations 2:2, 5:

> Without pity the Lord has swallowed up all the dwellings of Jacob; in his wrath he has torn down the strongholds of the Daughter of Judah. He has brought her kingdom and its princes down to the ground in dishonor.... The Lord is like an enemy; he has swallowed up Israel. He has swallowed up all her palaces and destroyed her strongholds. He has multiplied mourning and lamentation for the Daughter of Judah.

But His wrath is not separate from His love. In Micah 5 we learn of the promised Ruler who would come from Bethlehem. Here we see God, through the work of the promised Messiah, bringing back and restoring what had been lost:

> "I will destroy your horses from among you and demolish your chariots. I will destroy the cities of your land and tear down all your strongholds. I will destroy your witchcraft and you will no longer cast spells."

> Micah 5:10–12

God is plundering all that has become a false stronghold in the lives of His people.

4. We, Too, Are to Demolish Strongholds

When God's position as stronghold of His people has been destroyed through our fallen stewardship and disobedience, and after we are restored through repentance, we join in the fight to plunder the enemy's camp and win back what rightfully belongs to God. We call this spiritual warfare, and it is part of the ministry God has entrusted to His Church.

This, it would seem, is what Jesus is implying in Luke 11:21, after He cast out a demon:

> "When a strong man, fully armed, guards his own house, his possessions are safe. But when someone stronger attacks and overpowers him, he takes away the armor in which the man trusted and divides up the spoils."

Many present-day authors have used Luke 11:21 as an example of the varying degrees of demonic opposition (or demonic strongholds) that hinder the freedom of God's people. When we appropriate what God has entrusted to us in the Person and life of Christ and through the power of the Holy Spirit, we are told we have the authority to plunder and destroy the strongholds that blind people from the glory of Christ: "The god of this age has blinded the minds of unbelievers, so that they cannot see the light of the gospel of the glory of Christ, who is the image of God" (2 Corinthians 4:4).

Plundering strongholds is also what lies behind Paul's thinking when he explains, "The weapons we fight with are not the weapons of the world. On the contrary, they have divine power to demolish strongholds" (2 Corinthians 10:4)

The word for *stronghold, ochuroma,* occurs only here in all of the New Testament. But the Septuagint—an early translation of the Hebrew Old Testament into Greek—also uses *ochuroma* in Psalm 9:9: "The LORD is a refuge for the oppressed, a *stronghold* in times of trouble" (emphasis added). In writing 2 Corinthians 10:4 Paul is emphasizing the suitability of the Christian's spiritual weapons for destroying the strong fortresses of Satan, whether they are influencing individuals, a group of people or a particular geographical location.

Paul goes on to say, "We demolish *arguments* and every *pretension* that sets itself up against the knowledge of God, and we

91

take captive *every thought* to make it obedient to Christ" (2 Corinthians 10:5, emphasis added). The apostle is describing the demolition of fortress mentalities that would stand in opposition to God as the stronghold or point of reference for His people, whether individually or corporately. Again we can see the importance of thinking with a biblical worldview.

Strongholds and Stewardship

We have looked at some biblical examples of strongholds and recognized that the Lord wants to be the stronghold in the lives of His people. We have also noted that His people are vulnerable to fallen or negative strongholds—that is, anything against the nature and character and purpose of God in their lives. Now we need to come to terms with the manner in which strongholds are given access in our lives. The simple thesis is this: *Strongholds can be released, inherited or transferred from person to person, city to city, generation to generation.* We will discuss a few geographical examples of this.

Since we have defined a steward as someone responsible for somebody else's property, we must now go further along this line of thinking. In the last chapter we identified four major areas in which stewardship can become defiled, allowing negative strongholds to replace the stronghold of God in a given person, family, church, community, city or nation. In every situation the common denominator is *people*. What people think, do and say has a direct bearing on either the extension of the Kingdom of God or the resistance *to* the Kingdom of God in any given time and place.

The manner in which a steward looks after the landowner's property has a direct bearing on the fruitfulness of that type of stewardship, as well as on the response of the landowner himself. Jesus makes reference to this dual effect through such stewardship parables as the parable of the workers in the vineyard (Matthew 20:1–16); the parable of the tenants (Matthew 21:33–41); the parable of the talents (Matthew 25:14–30); and the parables of the sower, the weeds, the mustard seed, the yeast, the hidden treasure, the pearl and the net (all found in Matthew 13).

It has been estimated that 65 percent of Jesus' teaching in the New Testament is in parabolic form; 35 percent of such teaching refers to stewardship. Each of these parables is a commentary on stewardship that needs to be *redeemed* and *invested* so that God's purpose in the lives of His people can be brought to fruition. Each parable also gives insight into the impediments that hinder that stewardship from taking place, showing how it might be lost or hidden or stolen.

The Promised Land

The theme of the Promised Land is utilized many times in Scripture as a symbol of God's faithfulness in the lives of His people so they can enter the fullness He has promised them. This is the norm, starting in Genesis 12:1–3, when God assures Abram that He will bless him and his seed as he goes "to the land I will show you," prepared for him by the Lord. The purpose: that God can build a great nation through Abram, and that "all peoples on earth will be blessed through you."

As we trace the foundational aspect of God's covenantal relationship with His people, we find that the land God wants to give us becomes defiled through any one of the four ways we considered in the last chapter: idolatry, immorality, bloodshed and broken covenants. All this becomes the "cause and effect" on the land based on the particular stewardship of the individual. The land, as we have observed, takes on the effect or characteristic of the sin that has been committed by the stewards.

So it is that in Ezekiel 16:23–27, the increasing promiscuity of God's people provokes Him to anger and results in His *reducing their territory*, since as the defilement increases in a given land area, God's righteousness and protection in that same area are reduced, or even removed. Plainly this is due to the stewardship of the people. It is also a key factor (as I suggested in the last chapter) in explaining why church growth does not take place in certain areas, or is at best minimal, until land is cleansed from defilement and set free, in order that God's territory and Kingdom in the lives of His people can be extended.

A Warning from Joshua

Joshua 23 gives some key components with reference to the care we must take in the stewardship God has entrusted to us. Verse 5 declares God's desire:

> "The LORD your God himself will drive [your enemies] out of your way. He will push them out before you, and you will take possession of their land, as the LORD your God promised you."

Joshua continues, however, with these clear words of warning:

> "Be very strong; be careful to obey all that is written in the Book of the Law of Moses, without turning aside to the right or to the left. Do not associate with these nations that remain among you; do not invoke the names of their gods or swear by them. You must not serve them or bow down to them. But you are to hold fast to the LORD your God, as you have until now."

> verses 6–8

Then these sobering words:

> "... If you intermarry with them and associate with them, then you may be sure that the LORD your God will no longer drive out these nations before you. Instead, they will become snares and traps for you, whips on your backs and thorns in

your eyes, until you perish from this good land, which the LORD your God has given you."

verses 12–13

Later in Joshua's farewell words to Israel, he makes clear God's expectancy of His people:

"Now fear the LORD and serve him with all faithfulness. Throw away the gods your forefathers worshiped beyond the River and in Egypt, and serve the LORD."

Joshua 24:14

Joshua is trying to ensure that God's people do not return to the *cultural setting*, which affects them spiritually and physically through every form of idolatrous worship, fornication, immorality—indeed, anything contrary to the spiritual, physical and material lifestyle God established as a standard for His people. Clearly God longs to reign as His people's stronghold. He is warning them through Joshua that other strongholds will easily overtake them if they remove their allegiance from Him as their God and associate themselves with cultural and spiritual ways of the surrounding enemy nations.

Holy unto the Lord

Through the redemption, or winning back, of fallen stewardship (see Leviticus 25:24–25), God is causing His people to inherit what He has prepared for them.

Scripture speaks regularly about this inheritance. In most cases it is in reference to land, since as land is cleansed, the people who dwell in it are set free from the bondages and negative mindsets that blind them from God's purposes in their lives. As David puts it in Psalm 37:29, 34: "The righteous will inherit the land and dwell in it forever. . . . Wait for the LORD and keep his way. He will exalt you to inherit the land; when the wicked are cut off, you will see it." God is very particular in the lives of His people and chooses not to share His stewardship with anyone else!

In Leviticus 20:26 God declares, "You are to be holy to me because I, the LORD, am holy, and I have set you apart from the nations to be my own." This theme continues into Jeremiah 1:10: "See, today I appoint you over nations and kingdoms to uproot and tear down, to destroy and overthrow, to build and to plant." Doesn't this resemble Paul's comment that "the weapons we fight with . . . have divine power to demolish strongholds" (2 Corinthians 10:4)? Any stronghold opposing the stronghold of God needs to be uprooted and torn down, destroyed and overthrown, in order for God's righteous stronghold to be placed in the lives of His people.

A ministry team from the Joshua Connection was asked to pray with the pastors and elders of an influential church in Canada.[16] In years past this church was a leading light for evangelism and outreach. But a lack of accountability among the leadership and a questionable form of bookkeeping soon developed into a series of problems that affected and afflicted most in the fellowship. The church was now in significant debt. It owed money to former members. Immorality had taken place among the leadership. And membership was at an all-time low. It was not hard to sense the despair, discouragement and negativity as we entered the front door.

As we began to pray with the leadership, a number of issues were addressed, including issues of avarice and greed, the cover-up of sin and other unjustifiable, unholy practices that had been afflicting this church for several years. Following the confession and repentance of these practices, strongholds were broken in faith, and unholy alliances and allegiances removed. We declared healing and holiness into every component of that church's life.

Several days later a new sense of holiness and authority was evident in church services. A vast sum of money was suddenly released from previously unknown sources that eradicated the menacing financial debt. Fresh vision and excitement returned to the entire church family, and new people began attending the services. These were just the initial results in a church that sought the holiness and integrity of the Lord in its midst. It was now under the stronghold of the Lord and was entering its inheritance! In recent conversation with the pastors of that church, I learned that it is going literally from strength to strength in the leadership of the corporate Church in the city.

When unholiness goes either undetected or ignored, alternate strongholds invariably become a reality. God is a holy God and will not coexist with any form of unholiness.

The first verses of Ezra 9 express the sin of God's people in intermarriage:

> "The people of Israel, including the priests and the Levites, have not kept themselves separate from the neighboring peoples with their detestable practices. . . . They have taken some of their daughters as wives for themselves and their sons, and have *mingled the holy race* with the peoples around them. And the leaders and officials have led the way in this unfaithfulness."
>
> verses 1–2, emphasis added

Ezra confesses, on behalf of the people, their disregard for the commands given through the prophets sent by God, who had said:

> "The land you are entering to possess is a land polluted by the corruption of its peoples. By their detestable practices they have filled it with their impurity from one end to the other. Therefore, do not give your daughters in marriage to their sons or take their daughters for your sons. Do not seek a treaty of friendship with them at any time, that you may be strong and eat the good things of the land and leave it to your children as an everlasting inheritance."
>
> verses 11–12

This might appear something of an "ethnic cleansing" in the mind of God. But we must recall that He is a holy God and we, too, are called to be holy: "Just as he who called you is holy, so be holy in all you do; for it is written: 'Be holy, because I am holy'" (1 Peter 1:15–16; see Leviticus 11:44–45). Peter makes clear that we are "the people of God" (1 Peter 2:10), called to reflect His character in our lives, marriages, work and worship. We are to be "living letters."

Generational Stewardship

Unholiness in the lives of God's people removes His standard of righteousness, and Him as their stronghold.

In studying this theme over the last several years, we have been able to identify at least five main ways that stewardship, either positive or negative, is passed on from person to person, family to family and generation to generation. Through procreation, and the subsequent act of being born into this world, children inherit the ways of their foreparents. This means that sin and defilement become generational.

The stewardship we inherit by birth is subject to defilement because we are born into a fallen world—a world that has estranged itself from God as the stronghold of protection and righteousness. The apostle Peter alluded to "the empty way of life handed down to you from your forefathers" (1 Peter 1:18).

Here are five areas of our physical and spiritual inheritance, all of which are ways strongholds are passed on to us.

1. Genetic Inheritance

Our genetic inheritance includes the passing on of certain physical characteristics and aptitudes. Some of these traits, through the sin of past generations, can become distorted, resulting in illnesses or deformity. These require the healing and deliverance of the Lord for the severing of the sinful bloodline of stewardship.

2. Heredity

Similar to our genetic inheritance, heredity includes the passing on of social, mental, emotional or spiritual attitudes that can be observed from one generation to another. There can be good heredity and distorted heredity, begetting from one generation to another what is both good and bad, based on the content and quality of our foreparents' stewardship.

3. Psychic Inheritance

Our psychic inheritance refers to the fallen part of our spiritual natures. When a person is born again of the Holy Spirit, his or her spirit is activated or reborn through the Spirit. Since we are all born into this world with the capacity and desire for worship, even the non-Christian is attracted to spiritual reality. Today we observe the increase of New Age and shaman-based religions throughout the world, even though we may not realize it is people's fallen spiritual natures—their psychic inheritance—calling out from within them to be fulfilled.

4. Occult Inheritance

Our occult inheritance is similar to the psychic, but it includes actual willing involvement in specific occultic activities too numerous to name. This means being involved in anything that is hidden from, and contrary to, the holy purposes of God. Today even many Christians are involved in a variety of forms of the occult—horoscopes are one example—justifying it as harmless, or even acceptable to God.

5. Social and Cultural Inheritance

This involves the environment in which people are raised that influences their ways of thinking and acting and reacting in society. It can become a vehicle for their identity, out of which comes a variety of mindsets and perspectives that influence and dictate their attitudes and outlooks.

As a young boy in Scotland, I was told never to go near gypsies since they would most likely kidnap me! This warning was based purely on parental concern for me not to associate with people unknown to my family; but I actually lived out that false perception in the way I regarded gypsies, until it was dealt with through prayer when I was in my early twenties. Such can be the strength of one's environment in those early, formative years of life. Often the way we relate to issues and react to people is based on those earlier influences. Incidentally I have met some wonderful gypsy folk over the years, but until my earlier mindset was addressed, my perception of them was tainted.

Transference of Strongholds

Strongholds are subject to all these forms of generational stewardship. And since cities are composed of people, the makeup of people has a *direct effect* as well as an *influence* on the overall makeup of any urban setting, and its respective communities.

Strongholds that are received and transferred from person to person are *transferable* to churches and communities and cities and nations, based on the stewardship issues that characterize the people who compose the population. This was a major concern throughout the Old Testament. Leviticus 18:24–28, which we looked at in chapter 2, warned against sexual defilement, since land that is defiled must be "punished . . . for its sin" and the people "vomited out." Ezra 9:11–12, which we looked at in the last section, warned against unholy or "mixed" marriages.

God knew His people would be easily influenced through the thinking, practices and traditions of foreigners, which would cause them and their children to enter into sin and disobedience. A child receives influence from both paternal and maternal backgrounds; and unconfessed and unresolved sin, from either or both backgrounds, can result in a subsequent curse due to unholiness and the possibility of spiritual infestation.

The stewardship of our inheritance, both received and passed on, is critical in the eyes of the Lord. It was for this reason that the stewardship of one's life became an important factor in the New Testament Church, and why people were instructed and encouraged to live in a way that brought honor and glory to God.

According to Leviticus 26:40–42:

> "If they will confess their sins and the sins of their fathers—their treachery against me and their hostility toward me, which made me hostile toward them so that I sent them into the land of their enemies—then when their uncircumcised hearts are humbled and they pay for the sin, I will remember my covenant with Jacob and my covenant with Isaac and my covenant with Abraham, and I will *remember the land*."

> emphasis added

Roots, Reactions and Reflections of Nations

We are learning that the people who live in a nation reflect both the weaknesses and the strengths of their particular cultures. A nation can have sinful or fallen characteristics according to its history.

For example, we can distinguish quickly between nations that have been conquerors, such as the English, and those that have been conquered, such as the Scottish, the Irish and the Dutch. Indeed, political resentments seen today by the Scots or the Irish toward the English really have spiritual roots, since man is basically a spiritual being made in the image of God, who is a Spirit.

It is much more complicated than what might appear on the surface, since many characteristics within nationalities are

101

in conflict. The tribal history of Scotland, my country of origin, reveals clans that conquer and clans that have been conquered, with all the emotional and social reactions that follow. Add to that the class system, whether social or monetary, and other factors that create attitudes going back many generations, and the picture is complex indeed.

When the Selkirk settlers left Scotland, for example, transferring their stewardship to various parts of Canada and intermarrying with the Métis, the result was a mixture of sorrow, sadness, despair and spiritual confusion, which can still be found in several parts of Canada and the United States today. Yet behind this lay an earlier foundation of spiritual influence. Much of this is due to the Celtic influence found in the cultural background of many people groups that transferred their stewardship to other parts of the world.

Today we note a growing trend toward reclaiming many of the positive aspects of the Celtic influence on Christianity—and it is important to state that there *are* many positive influences. A much earlier form of Celtic influence, however, has a troubling pedigree. Let's take a look at it, since it illustrates the transfer of a religious stronghold that has had a significant effect on present-day culture.

Celtic Spiritual History

The New Webster's Dictionary and Thesaurus of the English Language defines a Celt as one of the ancient peoples speaking Celtic. Those people originated in southwestern Germany around 1500 B.C. and spread through France to northern Spain and the British Isles around the seventh century B.C. Successive Celtic invasions reached upper Italy, Bohemia, Hungary and Illyria in the fourth century B.C., and Asia Minor in the third century B.C. These peoples were conquered and absorbed by the Romans and barbarians until only Brittany and the rest of the British Isles remained Celtic.[17]

The spirituality of the Celtic tradition is intimately connected with Druidism. Writes George Otis, drawing on the research of the British historian Stuart Piggot:

> The ancient Celts endeavored to depict the intelligence behind and within creation by personifying it. One of the ways they accomplished this was by carving grim-faced gods in rotting tree trunks situated in woods near natural springs. Even today people in Celtic lands "dress" wells with flowers and make vow pilgrimages to ancient oaks and special stones.[18]

Pantheism and animism play a significant role in the spiritual infrastructure of traditional Druidism. In his book *Dawning of the Pagan Moon* David Burnett states:

> Celtic religion and mythology is difficult, if not impossible, for modern man to reconstruct completely. What remains are stone carvings, burial mounds, Roman conquerors, and wondrous myths passed on by word of mouth to younger generations. The Celts lived in a mysterious world that supported life itself. Nature itself was considered alive, and watched over by the gods through lightly owed reverence. These gods were believed to inhabit waters and mountain peaks.[19]

Otis refers to Romans 1:21–27, where Paul the apostle connects nature-based idolatry and sexual perversion, and comments:

> By placing themselves under the influence of evil world rulers, [the ancients] found their imaginations darkened to the implications of violence and sexual defilement—a blindness that eventually led to a devastation of their bodies, minds and cultures. Anthropological and archaeological findings over the last several years have lent credence to the apostle's claims. . . . Celtic priests [are] known to have been open homosexuals or of ambiguous sexual identity. . . .[20]

Today's Spiritual Inheritance

When we consider the inheritance of the Celtic tradition with many people who have traveled to various areas throughout Europe and North America, we begin to see how the transfer of this religious stronghold has had a significant effect on present-day culture. Burnett identifies the Druids, for example, as one of the "most fascinating aspects of Celtic religion," and that "an important part of their teaching was that the soul did not die but passed into another body."[21] Such is part of the spiritual inheritance of many with Scottish, Irish and Welsh backgrounds.

Certain characteristic roots of Scots include aggression, violence and sadness. They may experience the latter while listening to certain Scottish songs and bagpipe music, because of the deeply imbedded memories lying at the heart of the Scottish people. Bagpipes, incidentally, may make some people weep at their sound, but hearing the tune of "Amazing Grace" accompanied by bagpipes is something not to be forgotten—or missed! At times the Scots may give the impression of being stubborn, yet often this is because they feel inferior and inarticulate, especially in the presence of English people, at whose hands they experienced severe oppression.

Stronghold Thinking

Stewardship plays a major role in developing and sustaining strongholds in a person's life. God calls on us to disinherit what is *not* of Him in order to inherit, or repossess, what *is* of Him. We know already from Scripture that God wants to be the stronghold of our lives—our protection, our citadel, our fortress and our tower. In other words, He wants to be our point of reference in every part of our being—spirit, soul and body. But our stewardship—our ways of thinking and living—depends largely on how we *think*.

Jesus was well aware of the power of thinking. After He forgave the sins of the paralytic, He knew some of His onlookers felt more than skeptical. So He proceeded to heal the man, saying to His critics, "Why do you entertain evil thoughts in your hearts?" (Matthew 9:4). He was referring to some of the teachers of the law who were accusing Him of blasphemy—forgiving sin. The thinking of at least some must have changed, since by verse 8 the crowd was "filled with awe" and "praised God" for what they had seen.

The apostle Paul, who wrote that "we take captive every thought to make it obedient to Christ" (2 Corinthians 10:5), also wrote:

> We know that we all possess knowledge. Knowledge puffs up, but love builds up. The man who thinks he knows something does not yet know as he ought to know. But the man who loves God is known by God.
>
> 1 Corinthians 8:1–3

Our thoughts are determined by the intentions of our hearts. Listen to Jesus:

> "Out of the overflow of the heart the mouth speaks. The good man brings good things out of the good stored up in him, and the evil man brings evil things out of the evil stored up in him."
>
> Matthew 12:34–35

Cruden's Complete Concordance to the Old and New Testaments defines *heart* as "the seat of life or strength; hence it means mind, soul, spirit, or one's entire emotional nature and understanding."[22] Only God's Word can judge the heart: "The word of God is living and active. Sharper than any double-edged sword, it penetrates even to dividing soul and spirit, joints and marrow;

it judges the thoughts and attitudes of the heart" (Hebrews 4:12). Jeremiah wrote that "the heart is deceitful above all things and beyond cure. Who can understand it? I the LORD search the heart and examine the mind, to reward a man according to his conduct, according to what his deeds deserve" (Jeremiah 17:9–10).

All of Scripture links the activities of God's people with their ways of thinking and living—the thoughts and the intentions of their hearts. Such thoughts and intentions become fodder for negative strongholds—anything contrary to the stronghold of God in their lives.

Mirror, Mirror on the Wall

We tend to see ourselves through the influence of others. If we do not see ourselves for who we are in Christ, we become vulnerable to the opinions and strongholds of others.

God promised deliverance for His people enslaved in Egypt, telling them of His desire to establish a covenant with them and to free them from the yoke of the Egyptians. But Exodus 6:9 shows the effect of stronghold thinking on God's people: "Moses reported this to the Israelites, but they did not listen to him *because of their discouragement and cruel bondage*" (emphasis added). The stronghold of their bondage under the Egyptians prevented them from truly hearing and receiving God's words of promise and deliverance. They could not see their true reflection as the people of God.

Much later the spies sent out to explore Canaan reported back with a wonderful description of the fruitfulness of the Promised Land. "But the people who live there are powerful," they added, "and the cities are fortified and very large" (Numbers 13:28). Even when Caleb tried to counter this negative thinking, the other spies declared, "We can't attack those people; they are stronger than we are. . . . We seemed like grasshoppers in our own eyes, and we looked the same to them" (verses 31, 33).

The thinking of the majority of the spies prevented them from possessing the land at that time. *Strongholds of fear and doubt had begun to inhabit their thinking, affecting their actions.*

The stewardship of those already occupying Canaan resulted in a geographical or territorial stronghold of fear and intimidation affecting those who would enter the land. Since ten of the spies had, in effect, allowed themselves to be intimidated by this stronghold on the land, rather than remain covered under the stronghold of the Lord, they could not "see" with His eyes, and so were immediately vulnerable to the resident stronghold thinking and influence. Thus they failed to bring back a true report, despite the fact that they saw and then returned to their people the fruit of this land, which was a sign of the Lord's promise on it—a cluster of grapes from the Valley of Eschol. Only Joshua and Caleb remained unaffected by this foreign stronghold, since they remained secure under the Lord, who was their stronghold, even in foreign territory.

When Our Thinking Became Corrupted

Such stronghold thinking developed in human beings following the separation of God and man in the Garden of Eden. In this setting Adam and Eve had walked and talked with God on a friendship basis. Their uncorrupted spirits had known His intentions and motives, and they had felt unafraid in His presence. Then sin crept into the agenda, which created defilement and separation. Adam and Eve could no longer respond to the heart of God, nor understand His intentions. From that time on, whenever God approached, man and woman misunderstood what He did or tried to communicate. Simply put, they misread God's motives.

Still today this can be the result when we break the covenant relationship of God's cover and protection in our lives. We misunderstand Him and cease to trust Him.

Mankind's stewardship thus became subject to the intense violation of corruption, which meant God had to withdraw His holiness from mankind's presence. This was due to original sin, as well as to ongoing sins of omission and commission, which affect us, others and future generations.

This explains God's intention in a passage like Deuteronomy 7, in which He commanded total destruction of the people whose land the Israelites were about to enter. Do you recognize the frequency of this theme? There was to be no intermarriage with them, and their ways of worship were to be removed completely. God's people were holy to the Lord, and He knew their hearts and spirits could be stolen through other cultural influences, which in turn would affect future generations. Thus Moses' clear command in verse 16:

> You must destroy all the peoples the LORD your God gives over to you. Do not look on them with pity and do not serve their gods, for that will be a snare to you.

From the first stage of creation, God planned to come to a particular people. To them, through them and with them He would begin to reveal His true nature. This is why He refers to Himself as jealous for His people. It is with them that He would share His nature and holiness.

Building on what we examined in the last chapter concerning the word *covenant*, we see that God initially came to Abraham and covenanted with him. Then He came to Moses, to whom He began to reveal His nature and laws. He covenanted with Israel that if they would be His people and be led by His laws, He would be their God and would give them a land flowing with milk and honey. He wanted to say to all the nations, "Look at these people. They model for you who and what I am. They reflect My nature."

God knew this would not work and that the Hebrew people would fail to be the glorious example He longed for. But He also knew they would lay the groundwork in *thought* and *history* into which His own Son, Jesus Christ, would come. Through Jesus He could reveal His own nature, once for all, and redeem mankind's fallen nature. The stronghold of the Lord would one day live in and be reflected from the very life of man himself.

How important to see ourselves from this perspective—in His image!

Sons of Zion or Sons of Greece?

As God undertook the process of creation for the first five days, we read that what He saw was good (see Genesis 1:4, 10, 12, 18, 21, 25). On the sixth day God formed man in His own image, breathed His own breath into him, and "the man became a living being" (Genesis 2:7). Genesis 1:31 states once again that at the end of the sixth day, "God saw all that he had made, and it was very good."

What a glorious revelation! Earth is redolent with the Spirit of God, who flows through all of nature. God has created man from that good, holy earth, and filled him with His own holy breath.

This is why the stewardship of God's earth is so important for us to understand, and why fallen stewardship has an effect on the earth around us. The way we think affects the way we live, act and interact with the rest of creation. Surely this is part of what lay behind Paul's thinking in Romans 12:2 and Philippians 2:1–5 in exhorting us to allow our minds to be transformed, and to think like Christ.

We do have a choice. Zechariah 9:13 highlights the conflict: "I will rouse your sons, O Zion, against your sons, O Greece, and make you like a warrior's sword." The biblical worldview of the sons of Zion comes from the influence of the holy God Himself. But the children of Zion have been in conflict (spiritually speaking) with the children of Greece for many generations. This conflict is apparent in the contrast of Judeo-Christianity with all the other religions of the world.

Hindu theology, for example, sees man to have begun as pure spirit in the heavens, then fallen to the "defilement" of godly incarnation. In this line of thinking, man must endure endless cycles of reincarnation—the wheels of *dharma*—always striving to renounce fleshly desires, so that the next incarnation can be in a higher caste. Eventually one becomes a Brahmin and can escape the wheels of *karma* and *dharma* to become pure spirit again, and be absorbed into nirvana.

Christian belief, by contrast, sees incarnation as an extraordinary blessing. We are redeemed through the work of Christ and are the sons and daughters of God. Earth, matter and the body are not evil but part of the good and blessed creation of God. It is our stewardship, rather, that defiles the land around us. That is what God has called us to redeem (see Leviticus 25:24) and win back for Him.

History reveals how the Hindu way of thinking has infiltrated many parts of the world. Today, then, we are still faced with Zechariah's challenge: Am I a child of Zion or a child of Greece?

We must never underestimate the spiritual power of our thinking. Unless we are willing to perceive and interpret reality with the mind of Christ, and through the direction of the Holy Spirit, our thinking will always be subject to the influence of the culture and tradition in which we live, and we will be sons of Greece rather than of Zion.

The Hellenistic period of influence still affects many people today, harking all the way back to 333 B.C., when Alexander the Great conquered the Middle East, and until the time of Christ and beyond, when Greek culture and thought dominated. Aristotle developed his thinking as a disciple of Plato, who believed (in a metaphysical refinement of Hindu theology) that all matter materialized out of the "ideal" or spiritual world. Whatever does not breathe, taught Aristotle, has no intelligence, will or desire. Spirit, if it exists at all, is different and apart from matter and human life.

This was never the German *Weltanschauung*, a comprehensive philosophy in which God's Spirit flows above, in and through all of life, and in which all creation has its own intelligence, will and desire. But when our thinking is not informed by the worldview of Scripture, and when we fail to understand Scripture in the way God intends, we allow for many varieties of negative and demonic strongholds to inhabit our thinking.

When we read that Jesus spoke directly to the winds of the storm and that they obeyed Him, our human thinking tells us that winds and storms have no life of their own, so how could they hear, understand or obey Jesus? We relegate much of Scripture to superstition. Sometimes we go so far as to demythologize it, stripping it of "myth" so we can believe it.

What Do *You* Think?

Minds that are defiled in this way find it hard to understand anything of the healing and deliverance ministry (among other things). Such thinking buys into the cessationist belief that signs and wonders, and the supernatural empowering of the Holy Spirit, ended once the early Church was firmly established.

This stronghold of thought is resident in many Christian denominations today. Historically we can trace the origin of such thinking and observe its effect on the Church as a whole. This stronghold has had a major impact on how the Church has grown (or not grown) in North America and Europe, in contrast to other parts of the world, whose mindset is more open to God's supernatural intervention in nature and in the lives of His people. Jude 10 says that "men speak abusively against whatever they do not understand."

Many leaders in the Church today—for example, proponents of the A.D. 2000 & Beyond Movement—believe it is

possible to fulfill the Great Commission early in the new millennium, giving every living person on earth the opportunity
to respond to the Gospel message. We, too, need to learn to
feel and think as Hebraic Christians, allowing God to expand
our worldview and thought structures to conform to the mind
of Christ. We need to be set free from the strongholds of deception that are corrupting our thinking and holding our minds
and lives captive. God is challenging us to be willing to *think*
according to a biblical perspective:

> Do not conform any longer to the pattern of this world,
> but be transformed by the renewing of your mind. Then you
> will be able to test and approve what God's will is—his good,
> pleasing and perfect will.
>
> Romans 12:2

Paul also instructs us in Philippians 4:8 to *think* about the
things that are true, noble, right, pure, lovely and admirable.
"Whatever you have learned or received or heard from me, or
seen in me," he continues, "put it into practice." How important it is, therefore, to have the "attitude . . . of Christ Jesus"
(Philippians 2:5) and "the mind of the Christ" (1 Corinthians
2:16).

> For who among men knows the thoughts of a man except
> the man's spirit within him? In the same way no one knows
> the thoughts of God except the Spirit of God. We have not
> received the spirit of the world but the Spirit who is from God,
> *that we may understand what God has freely given us.*
>
> 1 Corinthians 2:11–12, emphasis added

Because strongholds are largely formed from the background
and framework of our thought process, based on the history
and culture that have shaped the way we think, act and react,
we must constantly be on guard as the children of Zion against
the influence of the children of Greece.

A worldview from a Hebraic biblical perspective will allow us to hear the words of the much-loved Christmas carol based on the words of Psalm 98 from a new perspective, giving us a message for a hurting world:

> Joy to the world! The Lord is come;
> Let earth receive her King;
> Let every heart prepare Him room;
> And *heav'n and nature sing.*
>
> Joy to the earth! the Savior reigns;
> Let men their songs employ;
> *While fields and floods, rocks, hills and plains*
> *Repeat the sounding joy.*
>
> No more let sins and sorrows grow
> Nor thorns infest the ground;
> *He comes to make His blessings flow*
> *Far as the curse is found.*

Concerning the message in this carol, blunted by "two centuries of unbridled technology," Winkie Pratney writes:

> What a contrast between this earlier worship and many other modern works! Then it was heaven and nature would sound; today it is much more likely to be only heaven. Then the redemption of nature was bound up with that of men and women; now nature is isolated, ignored, virtually invisible.... We might call what is missing a Christian supernatural view of nature in ecology and environment. It has been gone so long few of us even know it is missing.[23]

God's salvation and the effects of His redemption will flow to the *whole* creation.

FIVE

PAST AND PRESENT:
OUR SPIRITUAL DNA

verything has a beginning. We know from Scripture that it all began in the Garden of Eden. In this geographical district God set into motion His plan for proper stewardship of the created order, mankind in close communion with the Creator. Adam and Eve were commissioned to care for this Garden, and in return they enjoyed extraordinary intimacy with God. The Bible tells of their walking together in the cool of the day.

Concerning this established order, Bob Beckett says:

> Even before there was an Adamic covenant, there was an Edenic covenant. The very first interaction God had with Adam, after breathing life into his inanimate form, was to set him within Eden in order for Adam to tend the Garden. . . .
>
> Before giving Adam any further instruction, even before giving him Eve, God established that Adam's responsibility was to tend the Garden of Eden. In return God would provide, through the Garden, Adam's need for food and a home. Adam's nourishment would come from the fruit of the trees of the Garden, and any shelter from the physical makeup of the land. This was the substance of the Edenic covenant, or "relationship of responsibility."[1]

With the Fall came separation from God, but man's connection with the land had already been established. The so-called "relationship of responsibility" meant that, for good or ill, human stewardship would have a bearing on the land itself and, once established, would remain embedded until a concerted effort was undertaken to change it. Thus, as we are seeing, people groups as well as individuals reap the consequences of decisions made, often generations earlier.

Man's stewardship travels with him. Strongholds are transferable! Man's stewardship includes his way of thinking, his way of living, his activities, his inheritance, everything that makes up his being as he travels the world, even from the time of what is referred to as "ancient pathways."

These pathways were really the first migration routes and points of entry into any given geographical area. Even at those early moments in human history, the influence of stewardship was at work, defined by who those people were, what their religious worldview involved, and what covenants and pacts they had established among themselves and with the gods they worshiped. Even these earliest roots resulted in fruit, both good and bad. In discovering the ramifications of this early influence, and its subsequent generations of stewardship, we learn what still may be affecting us today.

Sadly, much of man's stewardship is of a spiritual nature built on a demonic foundation. As we have already seen in the earlier pages of this book, mankind is in a state of conflict with the philosophies that inhabit the world as a result of our original separation from God. Unless we resolve this conflict, we will be kept from the state of intimacy that God yearns for us to experience.

It is not only our negative decisions that can cause harm. Recall Edgardo Silvoso's definition of a stronghold: "A mindset impregnated with hopelessness that causes us to accept as unchangeable situations that we know are contrary to the will of God." We might easily recognize the ways that such strongholds are developed in our lives through trauma. More subtle, however, is the fact that strongholds can be built not just on our weaknesses but on our *strengths*, which is one reason we do not immediately recognize them.

The Scots defending Edinburgh Castle were twice defeated by their enemies, the English, at their position of greatest strength. Edinburgh Castle was built atop a sheer cliff, which looks over onto Princes Street. On both occasions the Scots failed to place sentries at the cliff face, thinking the enemy could not scale the wall. Thus the greatest strength of the castle proved its greatest vulnerability.

Several times I have met with leadership groups representing a wide variety of denominations. The story is almost always the same: In the area of greatest strength, whether evangelism, healing, youth or counseling, came the area of weakness and vulnerability. Such issues as immorality, miscommunication and leadership indiscretion, to name but a few, became the spiritual Achilles heel that led to their fall or collapse.

Whether the lesson comes from Edinburgh Castle or from the breakup of a well-known ministry, the story continues to this day. Strongholds become established as points of reference for succeeding generations as we are influenced by strengths in our history, culture, sociology and spirituality. Anything not submitted to God, anything less than what He wants for His people, is subject to the exploitation of the enemy. And in the areas in which land becomes defiled through man's fallen stewardship, demonic activity is given permission to take place and flourish, if sin is permitted to remain and thrive and faulty foundations are not removed.

Transferring Strongholds

All of us have a spiritual inheritance. And that inheritance, in turn, tends to influence the way we think, act and interact.

During the summer of 1999 my wife, Marie, and I and some friends took a driving tour of Scotland. We spent much of the time studying the history of this land and how the influence of the early inhabitants of Scotland has spread to many different parts of the world. Scotland has an extraordinary deposit of ancient history, much of which is still visible to those willing to view the landscape with a special set of binoculars.

I read these words on a historic plaque near Ballymeanoth, near the area of Kilmartin:

> We can see many things in the landscape before us—the beauty of nature, the productivity of the land, a place where we feel we belong or a place we are visiting in passing. But there is another landscape here as well. It is an ancient landscape. It contained places for the dead, for ceremony and for ritual. For those who lived in this landscape, its history may have been sacred. As a representation of that sacred past, the landscape demands respect.

The signboard went on:

> The memory of a brave, brutal or compassionate act lives on in the landscape—in the clearing or by the stone or stream crossing where the deed took place. War leaves many such imprints in the landscape. The landscape changes as memories are forgotten, and new ones take their place. It looks different to the person who knows the landscape and its stories than to the person who does not.

For the people living in that part of Scotland, the landscape continues to influence the way they live, even if it is through the use of explanatory visitor centers. Memories from the past still influence the present.

Wherever people have lived, their spiritual DNA has affected the land, as well as those who subsequently came to live and work there. Part of this DNA includes components of life cemented in tradition and experience—both objective and subjective, negative and positive. Researchers such as George Otis Jr. believe that *trauma* leads to *pact*, which leads to *allegiance*. History often replays chemical tape recorders in our lives, and we become affected by the historic traumas of our family, social and cultural roots.

The Hollywood film *Braveheart*, for example, relived age-old wounds and memories between the Scots and the English—memories vivid right into the present day. Frank McCourt's Pulitzer Prize–winning book *Angela's Ashes* depicts similar wounds borne by the Irish. The power of bondage and trauma in one's culture can be powerful.

George Otis has shown that there is a formula of bondage for both individuals and groups as they travel the face of the earth over generations. Part of this formula can be found in pilgrimages and festivals that are, in effect, transfers of authority, based on fallen stewardship and demonic interplay, which are then transferred into new areas of domicile. Otis put it this way in *The Last of the Giants:*

> Evil spirits will generally remain entrenched in an area like Haiti or the Himalayas until their original invitation is revoked—an action that, unfortunately, is rarely taken. Whatever their education or outlook, people are almost universally reluctant to renounce events and systems that they perceive to be legitimate—if unflattering—elements of their own heritage. Consequently, rather than dispense with their old beliefs and customs, many societies make an effort to adapt them to contemporary attitudes and lifestyles.[2]

Otis goes on to say:

> While Muslims exchange their pre-Islamic heathen rituals for the Hajj, Hindus wade into the holy Ganges every twelve years for the Kumbh Mela Festival. As Europeans and Americans celebrate Druid paganism through Halloween, Brazilians lose their inhibitions to the frenzied and colorful beat of Carnivale. By repackaging ancient rites of spirit welcome and

appeasement as popular, and seemingly more benign, festivals and pilgrimages, the tenant rights of demonic powers are thereby reaffirmed by successive generations.[3]

Such is the power of our spiritual DNA, the past still affecting the present. Tracing the transfer of cultures and the movement of people groups over the generations, Otis has found that, as ancient peoples began to migrate from Babylon into other lands, their inherited roots—and resultant strongholds—went with them. These roots incorporated the genetic, hereditary, social, psychic and occult inheritance of their respective backgrounds. This changing spiritual territoriality shaped the new land areas of inheritance and developed into bondages influencing the way people lived and worked on the land.

Bondages: The Residence of Wounds

A bondage, by simple definition, is a distortion in an individual's attitude toward God, someone else, church, society or anything that might affect him. Through bondages, negative mindsets are released and strongholds given the right of access. Even Christians no longer think with the mind of Christ when their pasts afflict their present lives. Until such original or "root" bondages are removed, subsequent or prevailing bondages continue to build on the ancient foundations, preventing people from receiving God's higher purposes in their lives.

Wherever bondages are present, sin almost always has a foothold, since sin gives the enemy of God's people the right of access in their lives. The degree of severity of the resulting stronghold can be increased by demonic oppression, which in turn causes serious woundedness. The wounds springing from inherited roots may be emotional, spiritual, physical or a combination. And woundedness can become a spiritual atmosphere blanketing an entire community, affecting even those who move unaware into the area. A place might be characterized by a sense of worthlessness or depression due to long seasons of unemployment, for instance, or by a deep sadness irrespective of good local circumstances.

Once I prayed in a geographical area that bore a definite sense of despair. When I asked my host church about the most recent people group that had come to live in that area, they answered readily, "Vietnamese boat people." Even as they spoke, they became aware of the reason for the despair in the community, since boat people often arrive with nothing but despair. Their woundedness had taken up residence in the area, and a subtle stronghold of despair had begun to affect the entire community, including the church.

As I mentioned earlier, 1 Peter 1:13–19 represents an important passage on this subject, particularly verse 18: "You were redeemed from the empty way of life handed down to you from your forefathers. . . ." This means that the cross has made it possible for us to be delivered from the *effects* of inherited roots that are in opposition to our new lives in Christ. Several other passages indicate the extent of damage done by inherited roots, as well as the importance of confessing and renouncing the sinful ways of earlier generations that still affect us in the present (see Deuteronomy 5:9; Nehemiah 1:5–7, 9:32–35; Jeremiah 3:23–25, 14:20; and Daniel 9).

We should distinguish, however, between children *punished* for the sins of their fathers, which is not required by God (see Deuteronomy 24:16 and the parallel passage of Ezekiel 18:19–20), and children *suffering* the consequences of the sins of their forebears—an issue we will examine in greater detail in chapter 7. This latter principle is clearly seen, irrespective of religion, in groups that suffer from AIDS. All suffering and trauma needs to be addressed for what it is, since it leads others to react sinfully in their own right, thus perpetuating their inherited characteristics.

The bondages or inherited roots that lie at the base of transferred strongholds are found regularly in national characteristics and, more often than not, in family characteristics. A bondage to religion, for example, might become a pattern when the vehicle or power of that religion has, for several generations, taken the place of personal and liberating faith in Jesus Christ as Lord.

How Stewardship Shapes Bondages

We have seen that strongholds can develop for a number of reasons from the roots we have inherited as individuals, denominations, communities, even nations. It may help us to visualize this process if we study a biblical example, one in which we can trace the inherited roots back to their point of origin. The story of the Benjamites and King Saul demonstrates this well, showing the beginning of a stronghold that affected the people of God.

As the tribes of Israel were driving out the idolatrous peoples from Canaan after the death of Joshua, "the Benjamites ... failed to dislodge the Jebusites, who were living in Jerusalem" (Judges 1:21). God was not happy about this:

> "I brought you up out of Egypt and led you into the land that I swore to give to your forefathers. I said, 'I will never break my covenant with you, and you shall not make a covenant with the people of this land, but you shall break down their altars.' Yet you have disobeyed me. . . . Now therefore I tell you that I will not drive them out before you; they will be thorns in your sides and their gods will be a snare to you."
>
> Judges 2:1–3

Indeed, Israel proceeded to worship the gods of the surrounding peoples, which led them into lust, sexual perversion and male and female prostitution. Then came the consequences, as described in Judges 19–20.

A Levite was visiting Gibeah in Benjamite country. The perversion that had grown out of the earlier idol worship in the area led the men of the city to desire sex with this Levite. Told by the man's host that this was not possible, they raped his concubine instead. Based on what we read in Judges 19:28 and 20:5, we can assume she died from the horrific ordeal she went through.

All of Israel was inflamed at this event, but the tribe of Benjamin was unwilling to surrender the wicked men of Gibeah, have them put to death and so purge the evil from Israel.

Note at this point that *sin* had become well entrenched in the tribe of Benjamin. A *bondage*—a distorted relationship with God and with the rest of the tribes—had taken hold, and a distinctly *negative spirit* had now found its way into the thinking of this tribe. Indeed, a *stronghold* had begun to take effect.

In Judges 20 we read the sad account of all the other tribes going to war against their brother tribe, the Benjamites, and slaughtering 25,000 of their valiant swordsmen, except for six hundred men who fled into the desert. Judges 20:48 implies total destruction in all the Benjamite towns, which were set on fire. The rest of Israel gathered and "grieved for their brothers, the Benjamites" (21:6), hurt because this tribe had been cut off and feeling the gap the Lord had brought about (21:15) because of their sin.

As the chapter continues, we read of more suffering. Israel realized that the six hundred men needed wives, or else a tribe would be wiped out—but the eleven tribes had taken an oath before God at Mizpah not to give any of their daughters in marriage to the Benjamites. Then they learned that the people of Jabesh Gilead had failed to assemble before the Lord at Mizpah. So they sent 12,000 fighting men to kill everyone in Jabesh Gilead, including women and children—except for four hundred virgins, who were carried off forcibly into marriages with the Benjamites.

123

As a result the tribe of Benjamin was reestablished from six hundred demoralized, humiliated and defeated men, along with four hundred young women who had been bereaved and forced into marriage, and two hundred other women, referred to as the girls of Shiloh in Judges 21:21, forcibly removed from friends and family.

These roots would ultimately bear questionable fruit.

Many years later, when the prophet Samuel met Saul of Gibeah to anoint him the first king of Israel, the tall young man protested, "Am I not a Benjamite, from the smallest tribe of Israel, and is not my clan the least of all the clans of the tribe of Benjamin?" (1 Samuel 9:21). Later, when it was time to publicly make Saul king, he was found hiding among the baggage (see 1 Samuel 10:22). Even though he had already been filled with the Holy Spirit and prophesied (see 1 Samuel 10:10), we observe here a *stronghold of inferiority*.

We also see the outworking of the *inherited roots* in some of the events that followed:

- Saul could not stand firm before battle or before his fearful troops. He panicked and offered a sacrifice that only Samuel was permitted to make (see 1 Samuel 13:7–9).
- Saul failed to destroy Agag, king of the Amalekites, as Samuel instructed. He also became full of fantasies, setting up a monument in his own honor (see 1 Samuel 15:9–12).
- Saul blamed the soldiers for disobeying God and not totally destroying the Amalekites (see 1 Samuel 15:15).
- Saul again blamed the soldiers and made a "religious" excuse, saying he had kept some of the plunder in order to sacrifice it to the Lord at Gilgal. Again, blatant disobedience (1 Samuel 15:20–21; see Judges 20:12–13). Notice the hereditary pattern of refusing to accept responsibility.
- Hereditary roots—namely witchcraft, rebellion and idolatry—became the obvious factors behind the stronghold

that entered this tribe, affecting even King Saul (see 1 Samuel 15:22–23).

- Saul betrayed the weakness in his hereditary root in these words: "I have sinned. . . . I was afraid of the people and so I gave in to them" (see 1 Samuel 15:24). This suggests that the inherited root went right back to the experience of Gibeah.

First Samuel 15:17 seems to indicate, through the words of Samuel, that God's anointing on Saul could have enabled him to overcome this hereditary root: "Although you were once small in your own eyes, did you not become the head of the tribes of Israel?" But it was not to be. The Bible records the ongoing *effects* of the inherited root in Saul's life:

- Jealousy (see 1 Samuel 18:9)
- Attempted murder (see 1 Samuel 18:10–11; 19:9–11)
- Self-pity and manipulation (see 1 Samuel 22:7–8)
- Murder (see 1 Samuel 22:18–19)
- Terror at the sight of the Philistine army (see 1 Samuel 28:5)
- Occult activity (see 1 Samuel 28:7–8)
- Suicide (see 1 Samuel 31:4)

Looking at *strongholds* and *stronghold thinking* in this biblical example shows our need for discernment in ascertaining how much in an individual's makeup is of self and how much comes from a hereditary root. Notice, too, how the stewardship of one life in this example—Saul's—affected people in the present and in the future because of situations that arose from the past! This one biblical example reveals an important principle: *Strongholds and bondages left unchecked can become hereditary factors that will affect generations to come.*

If they are confessed, renounced and removed, on the other hand, our spiritual DNA can be changed, healing will be released and the negative stronghold replaced with the stronghold of God.

Roots and Fruits

In 1999 Marie and I were involved in a conference in the nation of St. Kitts in the East Caribbean. After I had finished teaching on the topic of inherited roots, a man approached me and asked if we would visit his property. He owned land in an area known as Bloody Point and described some serious problems. Besides the fact that people living in that area were experiencing a general malaise, resulting in depression and despair, our friend's productivity on the land was extremely poor, and his farm animals would often become sick or die, especially when young. But if he moved the animals from that section of land into neighboring territory, they would recover almost right away!

When we visited his property, the depression and heaviness were evident. A signboard erected by the Ministry of Tourism offered this description of Bloody Point:

> Nearby, on the banks of the Stonefort River, known also as Pelham River, both the English and the French settlers in 1626 united to fight against the native Carib Indians. Informed by a Carib woman, Barbe, of an impending assault by the natives, the settlers in a surprise attack massacred several thousand Caribs. It is said that the river flowed with blood for several days. This marked the end of Carib occupation of St. Kitts.

As a result of the bloody massacre of the Caribs by the English and French, the land was under an enormous stronghold. The historic defilement on the land would need to be addressed, and the issues of sin and its consequences removed, before the area could enjoy any sense of health and prosperity.

To be delivered, or transferred, from a negative or antichrist stronghold into the stronghold of the living God, *vicarious confession* on behalf of others is necessary, made possible for Christians through the priesthood of all believers. Peter put it this way:

> You are a chosen people, a royal priesthood, a holy nation, a people belonging to God, that you may declare the praises of him who called you out of darkness into his wonderful light.
>
> 1 Peter 2:9

Similarly Acts 2:38–39 refers to promises that Christians may legitimately receive on behalf of their children:

> "Repent and be baptized, every one of you, in the name of Jesus Christ for the forgiveness of your sins. And you will receive the gift of the Holy Spirit. The promise is for you and your children and for all who are far off—for all whom the Lord our God will call."

As we began an initial time of prayer and repentance, I could sense the beginning of change. Being British myself, I was able to enter into prayer identifying with some of the issues, standing in the gap on behalf of my people over the atrocities that had been committed for which they were partly responsible. Clearly a good deal of work still had to be undertaken after we left. But the participants familiar with the Bloody Point area testified that they, too, began to experience a lifting of the despair and hopelessness.

My experience in St. Kitts shows on a small scale how a prevailing spiritual atmosphere can characterize cultures and nations. Examples are not hard to come by.

Often one can observe in the lives of people who have Norse roots, for example, a sense of aggression, a usurping attitude, almost a Viking spirit. The English can give an impression of superiority toward other nationalities, yet at the

127

same time exhibit social inferiority stemming from a working class background. The Dutch can demonstrate spiritual confusion, since they have frequently been conquered and sometimes find it hard to define their identity. North American Indians often suffer inferiority, leading toward alcoholism, depression and other forms of social dishevelment. As the host people of a land, they have suffered intensely and undergone much offense and abuse at the hands of others. Hindus may experience strong occultic problems due to the nature of Hindu theology and its varying degrees of polytheism. The Huguenots experienced the trauma of being exiled, with their future generations often experiencing a sense of restlessness and sadness. Russians often suffer sadness as a consequence of their own history—a characteristic often seen on the faces of elderly Russians.

The Ukrainians also exhibit sadness, sorrow or utter despair, and are by their own admission people born expecting to suffer. Is this why people from a Ukrainian background can give the impression of being "negative positivists," hoping for the best but expecting the worst? I was told by the participants of a conference in the Ukraine that they saw their main gifting for the rest of the world as hospitality and generosity. They have been so misused and abused by others, however, that they find it hard to look forward to the future with any optimism or excitement. Ukrainians freed from such stronghold thinking become people with extraordinary color, flavor and diversity in their lives. When freed from the past, they enjoy a wonderful blend of realism and idealism.

Japanese women often reveal a sense of inferiority, while Jewish people emanate sadness and alienation from other people. (Indeed, they have been a grossly misunderstood and repressed people and the target of much persecution.) The Swiss exhibit a type of intellectualism, yet without leadership qualities. People from Acadia, a former French colony of eastern Canada, often give the impression of being unwanted or rejected, and they have little self-worth. Such characteristics can also be seen in the lives of the Cajun people (descended from the Acadians), as well as those with Acadian roots still living in eastern Canada and the Maritimes. People with Germanic roots reveal a sense of perfectionism at times and are often involved in the occult. Indeed, there is excellence in the lives of Germans, but if this is self-directed, pride becomes a serious issue.

Political resentments seen today by the Scots or Irish toward the English really have *spiritual roots*, which we see when we take time to unpack many of the issues that still exist today. The spiritual foundations at times reveal serious issues that give cause for the ongoing antipathy among these groups of people.

Furthermore the spiritual syncretism at the roots of many people groups influenced by Celtic, Druid and similar traditions (such as we looked at in chapter 4) causes them to suffer at times from *alien roots* and *poverty roots*.

Alien roots cause a sense of restlessness, a need for mobility either at work or at home. They also include a sense of not being understood; a sense of deep, unexplained sadness; a sense of not belonging in the local setting; and a sense of unexplained inner loneliness. At times such people simply keep moving on, with no real commitment to any particular territory.

Poverty roots result in the fear of hunger; a drive to feed the family yet a sense of never really having enough; a fierce desire to own land; a sense of inferiority; and a poverty of faith, self-worth, relationships and family life.

Our ministry teams have observed such character traits regularly in the lives of people from many cultural backgrounds over several years of pastoral ministry. Such people long for identity and purpose, but the sufficiency of God seems hard for them to grasp. Their inherited mindset blinds them to spiritual freedom.

Culture and the Citizenship of Heaven

So it is that each people group—indeed, each person—is, in varying ways, influenced by his or her unique cultural background. Though we have looked mostly at wounded or negative characteristics, let's not forget the good news! Positive traits are passed along as well.

In addition, the negative characteristics to which each culture is vulnerable can be neutralized or actually reversed through the process of forgiveness, renunciation and identificational repentance, so the positive character traits of each culture can be released and expressed. (We will look at this process in some detail in chapter 7.) When negative strongholds are removed and the righteous stronghold of God grasped, each person and culture finds its place in the citizenship of heaven. It is then that something of the true nature of the family of God is revealed with all its awesome beauty and diversity.

Strongholds are generational in character. But remember, God thinks and acts generationally. It has always been His intention to call all nations to Himself, so that as they live out their purpose and reflect His glory, the world can see that He is truly the Lord of history and King of the nations.

Scriptures such as Leviticus 23:21, Deuteronomy 23:2, 1 Chronicles 16:15, Psalm 105:8 ("He remembers his covenant forever, the word he commanded, for a thousand generations"), Isaiah 61:4 and Acts 2:39 are among those that highlight the generational activity of God. This is why it is important for us to try to think with a Hebrew mind in dealing with inherited roots. We need to look both backward and forward in the generations in order to bring about the power of the victory of the cross in the lives of those with whom we pray. After all, it is the Lord's desire for us to be *rooted* and established in His love, which will fill us "to the measure of all the fullness of God" (Ephesians 3:19).

Cindy Jacobs, co-founder and director of Generals of Intercession, emphasizes that not only individuals and people groups but nations and even denominations have unique giftings.

Although we experience denominations too often as sectarian strongholds, we might remember that they are historical manifestations of the work of the Holy Spirit in the early Church with powerful giftings that contribute to the Body of Christ as a whole. As long as each denomination does not limit its worship and understanding of God to its own denominational wineskin (which then can become a *comfortable* stronghold), the Church truly does become the sign of the Kingdom of God in the local community. True unity in the Body of Christ, seen by the rest of the world, bears testimony to Jesus' claim that He is God's gift of salvation to the world (see John 17:21).

Baptists teach us about salvation, while Methodists and Presbyterians inform us of social issues. Pentecostals share about the power of God through the Person and ministry of the Holy Spirit, while Nazarenes and Wesleyans testify about the importance of holiness. Roman Catholics teach us authority and the fear of the Lord, while the Anglicans/Episcopalians model the wonderful balance of preaching the Word of God within the guidelines of liturgy and worship. The heart of the Mennonite message is reconciliation. Sound biblical theology is a gift of the Lutherans. The Christian and Missionary Alliance folk can model what it means to have a heart for missions.

These are just a few examples of the extraordinary diversity within the Body of Christ. The more we participate in the positive characteristics of each tradition, the greater the proclamation of the Kingdom of God. It is time to climb on board for the adventure of a lifetime!

Just as with the Body of Christ, people groups and nations (*ethnos*) the world over also teach us about the wonderful mosaic of the people of God.

Blacks teach us about God's patient and longsuffering nature, while Hispanics and Latinos teach us about the family of God. Whites share about authority (both the balanced and the unbalanced or perverted use of it), while Aboriginal people have much to impart concerning the wonder of stewardship and the reality of the spiritual realm. Muslims teach us about the fear of God.

Once in Christ, the people of the world share a common vision focusing on the One who is the Lord of all life. Here is how John Dawson sums it up in his book *Healing America's Wounds*:

> Creation is more powerful than sin, more powerful than territorial spirits, more powerful than colonial legacies. If you have ever worshiped with Brazilians, you have experienced a joyous abandoned party in the presence of Jesus. The exuberance of carnival is redeemed; these people know how to celebrate being a child of God. I love the Italian commitment to family; I admire the dynamism of Nigerians and the hospitality of Egyptians; the nations are blessed with remarkable gifts—we need each other. There is no ideal world citizen or defining Christian personality. *Viva la différence!*[4]

This is why we need to understand in a contextual setting how strongholds are transferred from individuals to the communities in which they live and even into a wider field—the nations they choose as their adopted homes.

The English can teach us about the majesty of God, while Americans can inform us about the authority of the believer. Israelis can instruct us concerning the uniqueness of the living God who is above all other gods; Germans, about the excellence of God; the French, about His love. Ukrainians have much to share on the issues of God's hospitality and welcome. The Japanese reveal the spiritual warfare nature of God, while Canada's heart is for the healing of the nations. These and all the other nations of the world share an extraordinary destiny, as together we declare the glory of the Lord.

From City to City: Oppressive Strongholds at Work

Now that we understand the wide areas of influence, both negative and positive, that people groups produce as they move to and fro, let's look at another factor influencing the spiritual atmosphere of places. Quite simply, this factor is about evil forces at work. We will not be fully effective as the Church in our urban ministry until we identify the nature and extent of evil in a particular city, and perceive its life and activity through the eyes of the Lord.

This shows us the critical nature of our stewardship, for ultimately it is people who cause the roots of a city to be evil by allowing or actually promoting the work of evil. Even the city, as Jonah learned, awaits redemption! Let's see how this fits together.

The nine letters of St. Paul written to various churches in the Roman Empire are actually urban missives. Eight of the nine were sent to churches in principal cities of the eastern portion of the Empire—Corinth, Ephesus, Philippi, Colosse and Thessalonica, the most important cities in their respective Roman provinces. Each of the letters to the eight churches contains practical advice on undertaking ministry in that city and province. In each situation Paul's theology developed out of his attempt to instruct each church on how to carry on effective ministry in the city. It is all a matter of stewardship!

Paul was aware that each city was shaped by spiritual forces, and he warned the members of these churches not to be influenced by the powerful and deceptive strength of the principalities and powers at work there.

Review, for example, portions of his letters to Ephesus (Ephesians 6:10–12) and Colosse (Colossians 2:8). Christ had created spiritual authorities for His use in ordering human and heavenly society, but these had become corrupt due to the defilement of people's stewardship. Paul urged the believers, therefore, to resist being taken captive by every form of evil that could seduce them through thought and philosophy, and to equip themselves with "the full armor of God." Paul was aware of "the ruler of the kingdom of the air" (Ephesians 2:1–3) at work in the lives of those who were disobedient and who could influence others around them.

Concerning the influence of these spiritual forces inside the city, Robert C. Linthicum, in his book *City of God, City of Satan*, puts it this way:

The city is a primary battleground between God and Satan for both the people and systems of human society. Behind the seduction of a city's systems and structures, behind the principalities and powers that form the spiritual essence of those systems, behind the often dark and destructive angel that broods over the city seeking to possess it—behind these stands the shadowy figure of the one known as Satan. It is the "father of lies" who is at both the heart and the head of the city's seduction.[5]

Linthicum believes that a biblical understanding of a city's principalities and powers—and particularly the demonic dimensions of such powers—is absolutely essential for effective ministry in that city. He points out that the primary systems of most urban and semi-urban settings—the economic, political, educational and religious institutions—"have the potential to work for justice and economic equality for the people in wise stewardship of a city's resources if their functioning is based on both corporate and individual relationship with God."[6]

This in itself should give us the necessary impetus to pray for those in authority over us in our cities, so they truly seek the mind of God in the work they do on our behalf. In today's pluralistic society we need informed intercession to be undertaken on behalf of our leadership, which is a vital step toward effective community transformation.

The spirit of a community, city or nation is derived from a combination of the history, surroundings and systems that inhabit these territories, all influenced and determined by the people who have moved through it and the events that have occurred there. Linthicum believes we must understand the significance of this principle in order to minister to our cities accordingly.[7]

As we have seen with nations and people groups, each locality, city and territory becomes connected with either negative or positive contributions. Detroit, for example, is synonymous with automobile production. New Orleans is famous for Mardi Gras. Los Angeles is known for its film and television production, while Victoria, British Columbia, is called the Garden City of Canada for its unique beauty and picturesque setting. Nashville is known as the country music capital, while San Francisco is often equated with homosexuality.

How we view a city or experience its influence is based on its stewardship. Its stewardship, in turn, is determined by the stewards who live there. This is where our authority, as outlined by Paul, is key—not only for our protection, but for turning things around.

In *Taking Our Cities for God* John Dawson explores his belief that we can see the mark of God's sovereign purpose on our cities in the "redemptive gifts" in evidence there. He, like Linthicum, calls this concept the "soul" of a city. That soul shows that God participates in the creation of our cities and works for their redemption by placing guardian angels over them.[8] Second Kings 6:16–17 demonstrates this when God reveals His guardian angels to Elisha and his manservant in the city of Dothan.

As God's people we are "fearfully and wonderfully made" (Psalm 139:14). We are called to reflect His presence in our lives and work. As His stewards we are conduits of spiritual reality. It is essential that our spiritual eyes be opened in order for us to see things in our cities from God's perspective. The stewardship of our lives bears much influence on both today and tomorrow!

Contextualizing Strongholds

We have seen that strongholds and bondages can be part of our spiritual and cultural inheritance. While God plans to be our stronghold through the saving and sanctifying work of Jesus Christ in our lives, we live in a fallen world and find ourselves under entrenched patterns of thought, ideologies, values and behavior that, in one way or another, are contrary to the Word and will of God.

We have also seen how our spiritual stewardship affects the physical stewardship in the area in which we live. If our stewardship is fallen or negative—that is, contrary to God's Word and will—it may affect an area adversely. And cleansing our stewardship of its negative components will open previously veiled eyes to the Gospel of Christ.

Strongholds form a major part of our inheritance and are closely linked with our philosophies of thinking and living. They are subject to *relocation*, along with their "vehicles of existence"—that is, people.

In terms of missionary response and church growth, it appears that either resistance or receptivity to the Gospel in any given community is intimately linked with the strongholds that exist in the lives of the people in that community. If those strongholds and mindsets oppose the Kingdom of God, the people in the community will experience greater resistance in their understanding of the Gospel, and their minds will be blinded to essential spiritual principles.

But when that community is won for Christ and stewardship is redeemed, the light of the glory of God is released and revealed, and the Church can expand the message into the community. Kingdom growth *will* take place. Initially it occurs as individuals are transferred out of the kingdom of darkness into the Kingdom of light. Then in turn, through their witness, intercessory prayer and evangelism, resistance to the Gospel is reduced, and its influence increased and expanded.

As a demonstration of the importance of contextualization, as far as our spiritual stewardship is concerned, let me offer a personal example.

Many years ago I was called to pastor a small congregation of thirty to forty people. The average age was about 65. There was little vision or purpose in the life of the church. In fact, I was told not to expect much change because that community was composed of people who had come to the area to escape from everything, including the Church! Unwittingly I agreed with this mindset, and for some years I saw very little happen—mainly because this was my expectation, based on a false belief. In reality I was captive to a *stronghold of unbelief.*

The area was home to a number of ethnic groups, including First Nations people (native Indians). Some of them were Christians; others were involved in a high degree of native spirituality—shamanism and witchcraft. The focus of their spiritual quest was contrary to that of our church. There was also a degree of occultism and Satanism in the area, which the church had never addressed. Nor had the community or church really ever changed, mainly because individuals had never changed their way of thinking.

With an increase of intercessors in our congregation, however, things began changing quickly! We researched the area and learned how many people had immigrated there with inherited roots of antichrist and demonic thinking, thus rendering our evangelism ineffective. We realized we had been praying with almost no understanding of the needs of the community, so our intercession had lacked information and strategy. We could do little sowing, spiritually speaking, since the land was so full of rocks, thorns, spiritual birds of prey and other such hindrances.

Yet as issues were addressed, lives were changed, and we all began seeing our community from a new perspective. The community began to see the church in a new way, too. The veil covering their eyes was slowly lifted. During those years we encountered personal strongholds, church strongholds, community strongholds, cultural (native) strongholds and national strongholds. We dealt with all in exactly the same manner: confession, renunciation, deliverance from evil spirits and releasing healing into each relationship, whether individual or corporate. (Again, specifics on this in chapter 7.)

As we minister appropriately and accordingly, the boundaries of the Church of Jesus Christ, the sign of His Kingdom in the world, will continue to increase and expand.

Divine Transfer: Prepare for Change!

The relationship between strongholds and church growth needs to be dealt with on the micro level before it can be dealt with on the macro level. The Christian Church as a whole needs to grapple with the theology of strongholds as an issue that will not disappear since it is so earthed (as we have seen) in Scripture. We must think as children of Zion, not as children of Greece.

The witness of the Church must be the same as that of the psalmist David:

> The LORD is my rock, my fortress and my deliverer; my God is my rock, in whom I take refuge. He is my shield and the horn of my salvation, my *stronghold*.
>
> Psalm 18:2, emphasis added

David also put it this way:

> The LORD is my light and my salvation—whom shall I fear? The LORD is the *stronghold* of my life—of whom shall I be afraid?
>
> Psalm 27:1, emphasis added

This must surely be the aim of the Church—to transfer individuals and communities and nations from false strongholds into the stronghold of the living God, and to lead them into being changed from one degree of glory to another (see 2 Corinthians 3:18). Almost certainly this is why Paul confirms and encourages us with these words:

> The weapons we fight with are not the weapons of the world. On the contrary, they have divine power to demolish strongholds. We demolish arguments and every pretension that sets itself up against the knowledge of God, and we take captive every thought to make it obedient to Christ.
>
> 2 Corinthians 10:4–5

Understanding strongholds from this perspective gives meaning and credibility to the new tools of the hour—namely spiritual mapping, spiritual warfare and intercessory prayer. It helps us understand what commitment to the land really involves, and how our thinking, living, acting and interacting have a distinct bearing on our own lives and work and on the people around us.

This gives greater depth and clarification to our call as stewards of all that God has entrusted to us. We are people who release a distinct cause and effect—spiritually, relationally and physically—on the land on which we live. God expects us to become wise, diligent stewards of His divine real estate. When our stewardship becomes defiled and the land becomes cursed, we are responsible to address the issue.

As we keep all this in mind, it is now time to take up our position as stewards of God's land. We need to see reality with a set of divine lenses, recognizing what has to be uprooted and removed, and what preparation needs to be undertaken, so as to prepare for a rich and lasting harvest. God expects no less of His stewards.

SIX

THE CURSE
ON THE LAND

A religion of mere emotion and sensationalism is the most terrible of all curses that can come upon any people. The absence of reality is sad enough, but the aggravation of pretense is a deadly sin.

S. Chadwick

As stewards of the land, we need to recognize what is already at work in any given area that brings God pleasure and assures us of the blessing of His presence. Proper stewardship always focuses on the Lord, not on problems. Then He will reveal to us what does not please Him in any given area, why the problem exists in the first place, and how to remove whatever curse may be resident as a consequence of sin and defilement. It is a stretching commission, which is why we need to take hold of a solid biblical worldview.

First, however, we need to return to the issue of curses.

The word *curse* is not a very popular word in today's language. When we look at it from a biblical perspective, we often try to explain it away as something contrary to God's perfect purpose for His people. The word itself challenges our personal and corporate worldviews. But from a biblical perspective it simply cannot be overlooked. The challenge is set before us. Deuteronomy 28:1–2, for example:

> If you fully obey the LORD your God and carefully follow all his commands I give you today, the LORD your God will set you high above all the nations on earth. All these blessings will come upon you and accompany you if you obey the LORD your God.

The promises that follow consist of every provision that mankind requires for fulfilling his destiny on earth. Then Moses gives a solemn warning:

> If you do not obey the LORD your God and do not carefully follow all his commands and decrees I am giving you today, all these curses will come upon you and overtake you.

> verse 15

A careful reading of the many verses that follow shows the severity of punishment incurred by disobeying the commands of the living God. In the context of this passage, it seems expedient to note the detailed directions given to the people of God as found in Deuteronomy 30:15–20:

> See, I set before you today life and prosperity, death and destruction. For I command you today to love the LORD your God, to walk in his ways, and to keep his commands, decrees and laws; then you will live and increase, and the LORD your God will bless you in the land you are entering to possess.
>
> But if your heart turns away and you are not obedient, and if you are drawn away to bow down to other gods and worship them, I declare to you this day that you will certainly be destroyed. You will not live long in the land you are crossing the Jordan to enter and possess.

This day I call heaven and earth as witnesses against you that *I have set before you life and death, blessings and curses.* Now choose life, so that you and your children may live and that you may love the LORD your God, listen to his voice, and hold fast to him. For the LORD is your life, and he will give you many years in the land he swore to give to your fathers, Abraham, Isaac and Jacob.

emphasis added

Why Land Is Cursed

In the introduction to their book *The Breaking of Curses*, Frank and Ida Mae Hammond point out that the word *curse* is found in its various forms—six different words in Hebrew and three in Greek—more than 230 times in the Bible.[1]

The Hebrew word for *curse*, *arar*, means "to bind with a spell, to encircle with obstacles, to render powerless or to make infertile." The dictionary definition of *curse* includes "expressing or feeling abhorrence toward something." Another interpretation is "calling forth mischief or injury on someone or something else." In its simplest form the word *curse* merely means the removal of God's favor and presence from His people. In Genesis 3:14 *curse* is used with reference to man, while Genesis 3:17 uses it with reference to the ground. As the Hammonds put it, "A curse is a sentence of divine judgment on sinners. It is the opposite of covenantal blessing."[2]

We have seen that our stewardship—our custodianship of all that God has entrusted to us—is subject to defilement by our actions. From a pastoral perspective it is easy to observe that many people lack God's blessing in their lives. Something is preventing them from experiencing the abundant life as promised in Scripture. As we fail to bring God glory and honor, we reject His blessing on our lives, and also on what He has given us to care for.

Beckett writes in *Commitment to Conquer:*

> Curses are more than merely wishing evil on someone.... Curses convey spiritual power, particularly if the curses are invoked by occult practices that include sacrifice, voodoo or other forms of magic. Let me be quick to point out, however, that not every curse results in demonization.[3]

Every curse does result, however, in the hindrance of God's holy presence, and the result is always the opposite of God's blessing and favor. Beckett goes on to explain:

> Curses can be directed toward whole cities and regions and have real power over the community. Cindy Jacobs told me some years back that people involved in the occult can actually obtain catalogs of statues intended for use in cities. A person wishing to curse a city can purchase any number of statues, based on what kinds of curses they want to place on that city. What an open invitation for evil spirits to enter a territory![4]

It is important, therefore, for gatekeepers and watchmen to remain faithful to their responsibilities in caring for and protecting the land.

The book of Ezra tells about the return of the Jewish people from their exile in Babylon, as well as about rebuilding the Temple. After the Temple was dedicated in 516 B.C., Ezra wanted to teach the people everything involved in observing the Law, so that their relationship with God could be observed by other nations. The book of Ezra testifies to the purity and holiness required of God's people. Ezra 9:12 makes it abundantly clear, for instance (as we have noted from earlier in the Old Testament), that God forbade intermingling between Israel and any other group, due to the dangers involved in mixed marriages.

Ezra was aware of the magnitude of the sin of God's people, which had resulted in their exile and captivity (see Ezra

9:5–7). Both they and the work of their hands had become defiled because of their detestable practices, and Ezra was determined that this not happen again. God's people were to be "holy to the LORD" (Deuteronomy 7:6). Yet the Old Testament is full of examples in which God's people continued to defile the land around them through their sin. Their idolatrous worship and immorality were an abomination in God's sight, and their poor stewardship literally polluted the land. (Recall Leviticus 18:25–28 and Numbers 35:33.)

Jeremiah 7:20 provides some descriptive details of land that is cursed, along with those who dwell on it. God says, "My anger and my wrath will be poured out on this place, on man and beast, on the trees of the field and on the fruit of the ground, and it will burn and not be quenched." Verse 32 of the same chapter refers to a Valley of Slaughter, due to the fact that people would bury the dead in Topheth "until there is no more room. . . . *The land will become desolate*" (verses 32, 34, emphasis added).

The prophet Jeremiah asks: "How long will the land lie parched and the grass in every field be withered? Because those who live in it are wicked, the animals and birds have perished" (Jeremiah 12:4). Verse 11 refers to the land becoming a wasteland "because there is no one who cares." Man's disobedience has left the earth consumed by a curse. The people and whatever they have been put in charge of must bear the consequences of their guilt. But verse 15 of the same chapter points out that it is still God's overall desire to have compassion on His people and "bring each of them back to his own inheritance and his own country."

God Loves His Creation

Land is subject to the curse of man's disobedience and fallen stewardship. In chapter 3 we noted that this normally occurs in four categories of sin—idolatrous worship, sexual immorality, untimely bloodshed and broken covenants—and that the result of such fallen stewardship invokes God's wrath and judgment through war, famine, disease and ecological devastation.

Yet God loves His earth:

> For by [Jesus] all things were created: things in heaven and on earth, visible and invisible, whether thrones or powers or rulers or authorities; all things were created by him and for him.
>
> Colossians 1:16

In his revelation St. John echoes these words in the worship of the 24 elders:

> "You are worthy, our Lord and God, to receive glory and honor and power, for you created all things, and by your will they were created and have their being."
>
> Revelation 4:11

God created land for the purposes of revealing the goodness of His nature and character: "God called the dry ground 'land,' and the gathered waters he called 'seas.' And God saw that it was good" (Genesis 1:10). It makes sense, therefore, for Him to be "jealous for his land" (Joel 2:18)—or, as the Touchstone Bible puts it, "indignant for the honor of his land"—because of its great potential for Him and for His people. Little wonder, then, that God weeps over His land (see Jeremiah 9:10) and calls His people to work on it and take care of it (see Genesis 2:15; Psalm 115:16).

Not only God grieves—we find many examples throughout Scripture of mourning over failure to care for the land: "The merchants of the earth will weep and mourn over her because no one buys their cargoes any more" (Revelation 18:11). In addition: "They will sow wheat but reap thorns; they will wear themselves out but gain nothing. So bear the shame of your harvest because of the LORD's fierce anger" (Jeremiah 12:13). And Paul expressed in emotional words the anguish of creation itself, revealing an issue heavy on his heart:

> The creation waits in eager expectation for the sons of God to be revealed. For the creation was subjected to frustration, not by its own choice, but by the will of the one who subjected it, in hope that the creation itself will be liberated from its *bondage* to decay and brought into the glorious freedom of the children of God.
>
> We know that *the whole creation has been groaning* as in the pains of childbirth right up to the present time.
>
> Romans 8:19–22, emphasis added

No doubt these words stretch and challenge our worldview! It is almost as if the ground appears to have a will of its own. The point is, curses and bondages on the land do exist. But there is an even greater truth: We as God's stewards have the responsibility and authority to remove them!

The position we take regarding God's active, supernatural intervention, both in nature and in the lives of His people, will have a major effect on how the Church grows and develops in the world. In this context we need to ponder these words: "At the name of Jesus every knee should bow, in heaven and on earth and under the earth" (Philippians 2:10). Ultimately the Lord will be honored and glorified at *every* level of creation.

Let's see what the early Church did about this.

Rules That Protect the Land—and the Results

We have marked the connection between people's lives— our stewardship—and the effects on the land on which we live. We have also seen that fallen stewardship can be cleansed and

147

healed, allowing us to experience the release of God's promise and blessing. This in turn brings Him honor and glory, and His people the assurance of abundant life.

In Acts 15 and 16 we find the apostles and elders of the emerging New Testament Church dealing with crucial guidelines concerning the whole issue of stewardship—in particular, the effects of sin on the land and the judgment of God on land that occurs as a result of such sin. While the discussion involves whether or not to require Gentile converts to be circumcised, the guidelines reached by the leaders at the Council at Jerusalem are most revealing:

> We should write to [the converts], telling them to abstain from food polluted by idols, from sexual immorality, from the meat of strangled animals, and from blood.

> Acts 15:20

Here we find three of the four major sins on the land highlighted in one sentence: idolatrous worship, sexual immorality and the effect of bloodshed. Implied also is a warning regarding the dangers of breaking God's covenant with His people. C. Peter Wagner offers this insight in his commentary on the book of Acts:

> Why immorality would have been included in the list of sins is not entirely clear, except that Gentiles were, as a cultural characteristic, much more prone to immorality than Jews. In most New Testament lists of sins it is on the top of the list. In many of the pagan cultures, ritual immorality with temple prostitutes was a way of life, encouraged rather than condemned by society.[5]

We could take any one of the four regulations highlighted at the Council at Jerusalem as a clear directive regarding sin issues and judgment. Let's take its focus on food laws, notably as related to blood—an important topic of Old Testament guidelines.

Leviticus 3:17 articulates "a lasting ordinance for the generations to come, wherever you live: You must not eat any fat or any blood." Again in Deuteronomy 12:23: "Be sure you do not eat the blood, because the blood is the life, and you must not eat the life with the meat." Why was this ordinance reinforced at the Council at Jerusalem? Perhaps, according to Matthew Poole's commentary, "to teach them meekness, and to abstain from revenge. It is certain that such nations as feed on blood are most barbarous and cruel."[6]

The issue of blood involves not only the issue of what one eats, but also the issue of bloodshed between people groups. The account of the Council at Jerusalem in Acts 15 is an important passage, then, as we consider God's judgment on the land as a result of such sin.

The leaders of the emerging New Testament Church wanted to ensure that individual and corporate stewardship brought honor and glory to God as revealed in the Person of Christ. The topics of idolatrous worship, sexual immorality, untimely bloodshed (all types) and the breaking of God's covenant were crucial issues that the leadership knew had to be clearly understood and followed by the Church as a whole. Otherwise the land and the people living on it would be subject to the curse inflicted on the land as a result of their sin.

What was the result of the careful stewardship outlined at the Council of Jerusalem (teaching for holy and healthy living reaffirmed by Paul in his letters to the Romans and to the Corinthian church, as well as throughout the pastoral epistles)?

> As they traveled from town to town, they delivered the decisions reached by the apostles and elders in Jerusalem for the people to obey. So the churches were strengthened in the faith and grew daily in numbers.
>
> Acts 16:4–5

The result of their wise stewardship was exciting church growth! As God's people followed the guidelines for correct

149

and effective stewardship, the Church was strengthened and expanded daily.

Recognizing Curses

If curses do, in fact, exist, how do we recognize them? The danger is that we start looking for demons behind every tree and rock. Rather, we should focus on Jesus. As we do, we will become increasingly aware of ongoing impediments and obstacles that tend to block our effective growth in Him.

Ongoing and recurring problems that may have been involved in a family for several generations will continue to affect the people in the present generation. All of us form part of a continuum from the past, and our personal and corporate "ancient pathways" require thorough spiritual investigation (such as we saw in the last chapter).

Let's look at two areas of concern that can lead to curses being placed on people and land. These and other, related areas are worthy of significant treatment—indeed, separate publication—due to the depth of information and insight that God has given His Church about them in our day. As we look at these two areas, we must remember that we are doing so as stewards of God's land. What is not of Him, and what does not bring Him glory, needs to be removed.

Freemasonry: A Trojan Horse in the Church

Most people in the church have heard of Freemasonry and the Masonic lodge. Many who have been or who are involved with the lodge, however, are not fully aware of what their involvement actually includes. Many Masons become involved with the lodge due to peer pressure; others join because of family membership (a father or grandfather, for instance).

In their book *Fast Facts on False Teachings*, Ron Carlson and Ed Decker state:

> There are over six million Masons worldwide today. There are about 33,700 lodges and meeting places for the Masons. In the United States we have four million members and 15,300 lodges. Again, most Masons get into Freemasonry for business or social reasons, while others see it as a philanthropic organization of good works, or as a fraternal organization and a brotherhood. Many go into it out of pride, in the belief that through their good works they can save themselves.[7]

Several books have been written by Christians concerning the issue of Freemasonry, especially as it affects the Church today. Our objective here is to discover the *stewardship* connection of Freemasonry on the land and its effect on the people living there. In order to determine this, we need to know *how* and *where* Freemasonry falls under one or more of the four major categories of sin: idolatry, sexual immorality, untimely bloodshed and broken covenants.

Astonishingly enough, Freemasonry falls under all four categories! Yet for many years the Church has willingly opened her doors to receive this Trojan horse. Once inside the Church, the spirit of Freemasonry permeates almost every component of ministry.

In order to test the fruit of Freemasonry, we first need to look briefly into its history and compare it with Christianity.

Freemasonry Is Syncretistic

Albert Pike (1809–1891) has been regarded as one of the best interpreters of Masonic ritual. Born in Boston, he was a teacher and brigadier general in the Civil War. He held the highest office in Scottish Rite Masonry and rewrote all the Scottish Rite rituals still practiced today. These rituals are, for the most part, pagan and occultic in design. Pike himself was an admitted Luciferian, holding a belief that two coequal gods exist in the universe. Pike also believed that Lucifer was the god of good and light while Adonay, the Christian God, ruled evil and darkness.

The study of Freemasonry reveals that it is, in effect, a collection of pagan rites and initiations based on the religions and worship of Egypt. It involves worship of the sun god and includes just enough biblical terminology to deceive the unsuspecting. In his book *Freemasonry*, Jack Harris teaches "that the body of an initiated Mason is a temple, and together, Masons worldwide form a larger corporate temple of Freemasonry."[8]

This in itself is a revealing statement, especially when contrasted with Paul's teaching in Ephesians 2:20 that the members of God's household are "built on the foundation of the apostles and prophets, with Christ Jesus himself as the chief cornerstone." It is interesting to note that the headquarters of Scottish Rite Masonry in Washington, D.C., has these words engraved in stone over the entrance to the building: *Freemasonry Builds Temples in the Hearts of Men and Nations.* It would appear, then, that we have a spiritual collision between Freemasonry and Christianity.

Indeed, on this note Harris quotes Albert Mackey from his *Encyclopedia of Freemasonry,* under the heading "Bible":

> The Bible is used among nations as the symbol of the will of God, however it may be expressed, and therefore, whatever to any people expresses that will may be used as a substitute for that Bible in a Masonic lodge. Thus in a lodge consisting of Jews, the Old Testament alone will be used on the altar, while Turkish Masons may use the Koran. Whether it be the Gospels to the Christians, the Pentateuch to the Israelites, the Vedas to the Brahman, it everywhere conveys the same idea, that of the symbolism of the divine will revealed to men.[9]

Freemasonry is, therefore, clearly immersed in syncretism. Freemasonry considers its religion to be universal and thus does not recognize the uniqueness of Jesus Christ as the Son of God. Masons regard God, moreover, as a force in nature, not a personal Supreme Being. This, in itself, is part of the deception of Masonry, and effectively establishes it as a religion in its own right. Albert Pike says in his book *Morals and Dogma:*

> Every masonic lodge is a temple of religion, and its teachings are instructions in religion. . . . This is the true religion revealed to the ancient patriarchs; which masonry has taught for many centuries, and which it will continue to teach as long as time endures.[10]

Masons refer to God as the Grand Artificer, or architect, of the universe, a term acceptable to all other religions except Christianity, which makes it clear that Jesus Christ created the universe (see John 1:2–3; Colossians 1:16).

Albert Mackey in his *Encyclopedia of Freemasonry* states that "the all-seeing eye is a symbol of God manifested in omnipresence."[11] Mackey acknowledges that the book of Psalms refers to the eye of the Lord, but says that "on the same principle, the Egyptians represented Osiris, their chief deity, by the symbol of an open eye, and placed hieroglyphics on it in all their temples."[12] This all-seeing eye is incorporated in Masonic architecture all over the world, and also appears on the reverse side of the American dollar bill.

For all these reasons and many more, it is both a mystery and a concern that many Christians—and many Christian clergy—have belonged to the lodge over the years. The Church should be concerned by the fact that the Bible is put on the same level as every other "holy" book, and alarmed by the spirit *behind* Freemasonry. This ancient spirit has existed since the fall of man as recorded in Genesis 3 and the rise of humanism as found in Genesis 11. Freemasonry is simply another adaptive deception in which God is dethroned and man enthroned, and in which man chooses to eat from the tree of the knowledge of good and evil rather than from the tree of life (see Genesis 2:9).

If an influence from Freemasonry has been passed on from one generation to another, how does this affect not only the Church but individuals, families, the city and even the nation? In what ways does a root of Freemasonry reveal itself?

The Fruit Reveals the Root

As a pastor I have worked with people from different churches and ministry groups for many years. My colleagues and I, along with our leadership teams, have observed a number of consequences that come from Freemasonry (or any of its offspring and sibling organizations) that affect generations of family members. Some of these consequences are as follows:

1. The spiritual separation of husbands and wives through the oaths of secrecy, with serious consequences for the Mason and his family should he reveal information.
2. The release of lust in both sexes: for sex (including perversions), for power, for money and for control of others.
3. The release of sickness and infirmity in families, often through the words of the oaths made by the Mason. Several of the ailments suffered by members of a Masonic family seem to be directly linked with the graphic words used in oaths.
4. The release of bitterness and anger in women who tend to learn to control and manipulate in the family. Often we have found that women either become subject to a controlling spirit or else they become docile and passive and experience all kinds of illness.
5. The release of curses into the family and down throughout the generations—such as lust and uncleanness, illegitimacy, infirmity, death and destruction (especially for the firstborn son—the so-called Lewis curse).
6. The release of a curse of religion in which a form of religion is maintained without faith in Jesus Christ as Lord.

In cases such as this, we find that Christians who are Freemasons find it very hard to grow in the knowledge of Jesus as Lord and to experience the fullness of the Holy Spirit in their lives. It is as if they suffer from spiritual confusion. They also tend to disagree with godly leadership.

7. Difficulty for the Gospel to mature every part of the life and ministry of a church based on Freemasonry until the leadership addresses and deals with the deception as contrary to Christian doctrine.

8. The development of what we refer to as the "mirror image" effect. Leaders may see a problem, but before anything can be done about it, the problem reflects on them and they are blamed for it. It often results in the removal of their pastoral authority and in the desertion or betrayal of close friends and colleagues.

Since Freemasonry is syncretistic, secretive and somewhat selective in those who are chosen as members, it can have a detrimental effect on the development of any city.

In many communities and cities, the lodge is situated, physically speaking, in an influential location. It is invariably positioned near commerce and business—places involved with education, government and politics—as well as near Christian churches and cults. Churches built on Masonic foundations often experience trouble in relationships, decision-making on the part of the leadership, evangelistic outreach into the community, music and worship—not surprising when one considers the spiritual pedigree of Freemasonry! Other problems include financial issues, difficulties in maintaining youth ministry and lack of freedom in God's presence during times of worship. It is as if there is a sense of restriction or suppression denying participants the full freedom of worship that God seeks for His people.

Freemasonry is undoubtedly a form of defiled stewardship that needs to be removed from the roots of individuals, families and the local church. It also needs to be addressed at the roots of a city, if in any way the foundation and subsequent development of that city involved influential Masons.

While implications such as these could make us defensive, we need to be honest before the Lord and seek His counsel as to whether we or our families have ever had any involvement with Freemasonry. My comments in this chapter are addressed not at Freemasons but at the *spirit that lies behind their worship and membership*, which often goes unrecognized by innocent participants. Simply put, Freemasonry and the Christian Church do not belong with one another. In fact, they are totally incompatible!

A Hornet's Nest and a Can of Worms

Since many churches are funded, and at times founded, by Masons, this can lead to obvious areas of conflict in a congregation praying for transformation in its community. Putting it mildly, hornets' nests and cans of worms will readily appear! The conflict between two kingdoms becomes apparent.

Once our ministry team was asked to pray through a church that had been influenced by Freemasonry for many years. Serious issues of manipulative control had affected the pastor, elders and those involved in music and worship, as well as the areas of finances, youth ministry and community outreach. Anger, division and immorality had already wounded the church membership in a variety of ways.

When we discovered that several former pastors, elders and worship leaders had been involved in Freemasonry, the present leadership confessed and repented of this involvement.

The following Sunday an extraordinary sense of purity and holiness permeated the worship. Some weeks later a woman came to the pastor and complained that her "power over the community" had been removed, which she wanted returned, and she knew it was due to something the church had done.

It turned out that she was one of the city's leading spiritual-ists, and that her "power" was removed at the exact moment of our time of prayer and cleansing!

Needless to say, her "power" was not returned to her, and today this is a thriving congregation making wonderful inroads into its community. The problems in the church had repre-sented the wider community as well; and as these were ad-dressed, a new authority entered the church, giving it greater spiritual leverage in the area.

I have witnessed similar results countless times in churches that have had to deal honestly and prayerfully with this con-tentious issue. The evidence leads us to conclude that the in-fluence of Freemasonry, and the spirit that lies behind it, rep-resents a curse on the land due to the way it can affect the spiritual terrain of an area and the people who live and work there.

Toxic Power Lines: Truth or Fiction?

One further subject, while partly speculative, has become a topic of interest in both Christian and New Age settings. As stewards of the land, we must not take the ostrich approach and bury our heads in the sand regarding this subject. It is a developing topic of conversation in several church and min-istry settings today: the subject of ley lines.

In my personal library I have more than twenty books re-lated to the subject of ley lines. It did not originate as a Chris-tian concept at all. A quick glance on the Internet today re-veals a myriad of sources giving elaborate information concerning this phenomenon. The April 1995 edition of *Hemispheres,* the in-flight magazine of United Airlines, includes an article entitled "Moors, Megaliths and Magic." It gives in-formation on a network of ley lines criss-crossing Great Britain, linking the area's sacred sites of antiquity.

In his *Spiritual Mapping Glossary* George Otis Jr. defines ley lines as

> geographic continuums of spiritualized power that are *established*—or at least *recognized*—by the early inhabitants of an area. . . . Depending on the culture in which they are found, ley lines may be viewed either as conduits through which spiritual power is transmitted, or as demarcation lines for spiritual authority.[13]

The late Kjell Sjöberg of Sweden, one of the contributing authors to *Breaking Strongholds in Your City*, refers to cities and communities that are planned in such a way as to fit in with pathways of ley lines and power points, in order not to disturb any flow of psychic energy that may be present.

In order to grasp this topic with both balance and insight, we will look at it as part of the bigger picture of spiritual mapping and the stewardship of the land.

Alfred Watkins and the Ley of the Land

The person most often connected with the subject of ley lines in terms of literary study is probably Alfred Watkins. An expert photographer in the early part of the twentieth century, interested in various antiquities, Watkins spent much of his time traveling the countryside near Hereford, England. On one occasion, when looking over the rolling landscape, he was inspired by the idea that many of the antiquities were sited along straight lines. He called these lines *leys*. Later, when he studied the areas on a map, he found that his idea appeared valid.

Much of the rest of his life was spent in following up this theory. As J. Havelock Fidler says in his book *Ley Lines: Their Nature and Properties:*

> The antiquities [Watkins] found which conformed to this pattern were prehistoric mounds, camp sites, pre-Reformation

churches, castles, wayside crosses, old wells, fords, and some old tracks. In certain cases groups of trees seemed to be on these lines, and of great importance were standing stones and stone circles. Admittedly, not all these features could be considered to be of similar antiquity, but he pointed out, for instance, that many early churches had been built on sites of much greater age.[14]

We have learned from spiritual mapping in many parts of the world that fallen stewardship often abounds for generations in particular land areas. In fact, where generations of psychic and occult activity have taken place, we find with increasing frequency that the existing spiritual problems do not entirely disappear, even after ongoing ministries of prayer and cleansing. In investigating such areas, our ministry teams normally undertake research from several perspectives: historical, physical, cultural and spiritual. These are the different ways people interface with each other, and they constitute the stewardship of a particular community. Through this method we look at the invisible spiritual aspects of lifestyles that have resulted in specific, visible, cause-and-effect characterizations.

In seeking an answer as to how ley lines were originally formed, Fidler looks at two alternative explanations: "Either they are a natural product of the earth's forces, or they were constructed by megalithic man for some particular purpose." He goes on to describe what other researchers have determined:

> Paul Screeton, in his survey of ley line knowledge, suggests that as the earth cooled, an intricate grid of geodetic lines was formed, possibly magnetic or gravitational in character. Tom Graves suggests that megalithic man was aware of this and placed his 'needles of stone' over the crossing points of these lines in order to bring these forces to the surface for some specific and unknown purpose.[15]

Fidler later concludes that these ley lines do exist and that they are normally found as lines of energy flow in ancient sites and pathways used by ancient and contemporary man, often in areas where rocks and trees have formed "energy charges."

Perhaps a simpler definition of a ley line is "a line joining two prominent points in the spiritual landscape, thought to be the line of a prehistoric track." One non-Christian source, Neville Drury's *Dictionary of Mysticism and the Occult*, refers to ley lines as alignments of ancient megaliths, dolmens and stone circles whose patterns constitute grids of power. Other sources in my library affirm that patterns of psychic power emanate from these ley lines. They are frequently linked with the practice of dowsing or water divining.

Pathways of Defiled Stewardship

In the ancient world, as people began to move out across the earth, their culture, history, spirituality—indeed, all forms of stewardship—went with them. Invariably they set up altars of offense to worship the gods they believed occupied the land, water and various other elements of nature. George Otis points out that such fallen stewardship was perpetuated over the generations through religious festivals and pilgrimages, cultural traditions (including ancestral worship), adaptive deceptions (or syncretism) and through unresolved social injustices.[16] Through such inherited stewardship, the enemy of God's people has managed to sustain his foothold in the lives of many throughout the world.

If we are to consider the existence of ley lines from a Christian perspective, we need to see them as connected with the original idolatrous and pagan stewardship and worship of the land that has never been confessed, renounced and removed in the name of Jesus Christ. If this is the case, then the reverse is also true: The higher the spiritual contamination in an area, the greater the possibility that ley lines exist and connect defiled points of reference in the immediate and surrounding areas.

Ley lines show the pattern of intensity of fallen stewardship that has given the enemy the right of access to various areas related geographically. So when we find areas that seem subject to intense spiritual confusion, psychic phenomena, moral decay, physical sickness, marital and family problems or business failure, we look closely for the cause of such phenomena and the possible connection with ley lines.

When a given land area has become defiled over the years through idolatrous worship and practice, that place inherits an unholiness that gives demonic interplay a stronghold for control. Ley line proponents believe that ancient sites were designed to coincide with underlying geodetic (or geodesic) lines, and that certain types of rock and wood have a specific magnetic charge or spiritual energy that can be determined through dowsing or divining.

This may give us insight as to why demonic spirits can gain a foothold in the lives of people in a particular geographical area. Power is attached to worship; thus we can understand why God makes it clear in the first two commandments that we are to love and worship only Him with our whole beings.

Proponents believe that ley lines probably map much of the world, forming a spiritual grid that may have existed since the Fall. We know that Satan attempts to counterfeit whatever Jesus does. Thus, just as Scripture describes God's desire to gather us together in one Body, united in one Spirit, so it would appear that Satan is attempting to gather all nations to himself through his own particular type of "networking" (see Habakkuk 1:15–17).

This is not to suggest philosophical dualism. The wonderful truth is that in the end, all nations will come and worship the living God as revealed in the Person of Jesus Christ (see Revelation 15:4). Satan is defeated. But in the meantime the extent to which ley lines are able to affect certain areas of the world is most likely determined by the stewardship of people living in those areas. Undoubtedly the demonic can inhabit an area more readily when ley lines exist.

They form a spiritual grid, I believe, that provides "feeding troughs" from which the infrastructure of the demonic can nourish itself and be granted authority in any given area. Throughout the world, the pagan worship of native peoples in certain areas has almost certainly continued to maintain and further strengthen ley lines. When this is the case, it appears that the outreach witness of the Church, and in particular overt evangelism, is made much more difficult and less effective.

Discerning and Dismembering Ley Lines

What can be done about ley lines from a Christian perspective? The fact that they may exist is, in itself, a stretch for many of us! Evidence for their existence is extrabiblical, since the Bible contains no proof texts either for or against them. An argument from silence, moreover, is anything but decisive. Yet if the enemy of God's people has established a network over the land in which people, cities and land are all held captive in some way, then we need to focus on the Lord who is the way, the truth and the life, and seek His counsel. We must seek to discern before we attempt to dismember.

When repeated prayer over some problem does not result in eventual breakthrough, it seems expedient to adopt spiritual mapping principles and, under proper spiritual authority, seek the counsel of the spiritual gatekeepers in that area. They are the ones who corporately can serve an eviction notice to the enemy. When all the proper representatives are present, we can humbly pray and ask forgiveness for all that has ever happened generationally in that area—all that has been in opposition to the purposes of God and that has had a grip on the people who live and work there. We are standing in the gap between previous and future generations, affirming the authority of Jesus Christ, who "is the same yesterday and today and forever" (Hebrews 13:8).

After confession and repentance, we rebuke, bind and cast out whatever forms of demonic interplay God has revealed to us through our research and prayer, as well as through the witness of the people who live in that area or situation. Depending on the extent and depth of stewardship, ley lines may be in a contained area, or they can stretch for hundreds or even thousands of miles. Normally we have the authority to deal only with the local area in which we live and work and minister, but in breaking known power points along parts of a ley line, we are substantially weakening its effect in that area. This is called "fracturing" a ley line.

When a ley line is removed or "dismembered," it is prayerfully replaced by God's line of authority and protection in that area. Then the redemptive calling of the particular community is called forth by the stewards of the land.

The issue of ley lines needs to be seen in the light of a biblical worldview and with a series of checks and balances. It is important that we retain integrity, accountability and a strong prayer cover so that *subjective* reasoning complements *objective* reasoning.

Can the existence of ley lines be considered as a curse on the land? The evidence leaves little room for doubt! Let's take a look at the research and prayer undertaken in one of the numerous prayer initiatives going on in the world, and examine the conclusions.

A Case Study: The Bali Prayer Initiative

For several years I have undertaken research and field work on the topic of ley lines. If they exist, they are more likely to be present in areas of former idolatry and bloodshed—and, in many cases, areas that are still under the influence of the occult.

In July 1996 a prayer initiative team visited Bali, an island of southern Indonesia, at the request of Balinese Christians. The team was led by John Robb, director of prayer mobilization for World Vision International. He is also the present coordinator for the Great Commission Roundtable. Some see him as the Indiana Jones of prayer initiatives!

John and his team undertook considerable research for this time of prayer and ministry, working with local church representatives. Bali is a solitary Hindu outpost amidst thousands of islands of the Indonesian archipelago, making up the largest Muslim country in the world. Before the coming of Hinduism, ancient Indonesians worshiped nature gods such as the god of the sun, of the mountains and of the sea. They also invoked the souls of the ancestors, which ostensibly descended on large stones erected for them. Today the Balinese continue to believe that gods live in the mountains, rocks, trees, winds, birds, streams and lakes.

Such is Bali—a place that belongs to the gods! Bali experiences much black magic and witchcraft. Various sexual fertility rites often take place on the land. Shiva, the Hindu god of destruction, is worshiped as the sun god. Battles between sorcerers under the demonic control of Shiva are often lethal. The Balinese believe it is essential to maintain the favor of the gods; the word *Bali* itself means "offering" or "sacrifice." The people believe that great calamities will come on them if continual offerings are not made to the gods and to deified ancestors. Ceremonies of purification and offerings of blood sacrifices are necessary, therefore, to wipe away pollution.

Countless bloody wars between the sixteenth and nineteenth centuries, as well as continual shedding of blood for demonic sacrifices, have been a reality in Balinese life. Human sacrifice has been present, too, practiced during the *Eka Dasa Rudra* ceremony held on Mount Agong every hundred years.

Informed Research

John Robb concludes from his research that ley lines, or occult lines of power, are a net Satan casts over a population to maintain control and create an atmosphere of spiritual darkness. He cites Habakkuk 1:14–17, which speaks of the foe who catches humans in his net, "destroying nations without mercy" (verse 17), and Habakkuk 2:5–10. During the Bali prayer initiative, John felt that such lines of occult influence present there, were obvious in the orientation and connection of the temples and household shrines, all of which are linked and aligned toward the mother temple. This temple is called *Besakih*, which means "dragon" and which is located on the highest mountain, Mount Agong.

All temples are positioned with respect to a mountain or seaward access; family temples look toward the mountains, while kitchens and livestock pens point toward the sea. Correct spatial orientation is very important to the Balinese. Unless they know their cardinal points and are able to see the central mountain, they experience a sense of disorientation.

John's team found in their research that the water system was a further issue in which power and ley lines existed. All water in the lakes and streams flowing down from the volcanoes is ostensibly under the control of one of Shiva's consorts, Dewi Danu and Durga, who rules the Creator Lake on the neighboring volcano, Mount Batur. As male and female deities of the two highest mountains, they form a complementary pair, the gods of the island. The high priest of the area, or one of his fellow priests, ascends to the Batur volcano, where steam hisses from the vents in the rocks, to collect droplets of water. These are then taken down to the temple, mixed with holy water from living springs around the lake and given to representatives from the various farming associations.

Strategic Prayer

During the prayer initiative, these and other issues were addressed. Prayer focused on the unreached subgroups of the society, along with the needs of churches and mission organizations. A time of identificational repentance took place, dealing with the idolatry and covenants with false gods such as Shiva.

On-site prayer took place at various strategic locations, including some of the temples and places of historic massacres and bloodshed.

Then it was determined prudent to address a probable occult line of power linking the southernmost temple Ulu Watu with Besakih. Under the authority of Jesus the line was broken. The people involved in the prayer initiative asked God to reveal His Person and power to the Balinese.

Some weeks later this temple was struck by lightning and burned, causing more than one hundred thousand dollars' worth of damage. A local newspaper reflected on this incident with these words: *Why Did Our God Allow This to Happen to His Temple?* In another location in the mountains, following the prayer undertaken by one of the teams, falling logs struck two other temples. Besakih, the mother temple, has been closed to all outside visitors, with the exception of active worshipers, ever since the Balinese Christians quietly repented there.

At the end of the prayer initiative, John recorded that everyone, including the local leaders, noticed a change of atmosphere, with a significant lightening of oppression. The next morning an earthquake shook the island. Spiritual renewal began to take place among some nominal Christians, including the growth of healing and deliverance meetings. Unbelievers showed greater responsiveness to the Gospel.

Some of the pastors began meeting once a month for extended prayer, and when the Indonesian government later began to build a four-hundred-foot statue to the Hindu god Vishnu, the pastors were alerted to pray against this idol. A few weeks later the head of the statue caught fire and burned.

Navigating a Hidden Realm

Understandably the issues of curses, Freemasonry and ley lines stretch us beyond our comfort zones. Each of these, as well as many other issues that we have not covered in this chapter, require a good deal of balance as well as immersion in ongoing prayer and biblical reflection. We also need to retain a biblical worldview by which the power and expediency of the Holy Spirit can speak directly into our lives concerning issues that can be somewhat bewildering!

God is undoubtedly revealing things to us that up until this time have been hidden and unknown. These issues tend to hold clues that help us navigate the contours of what seems at times to be an indecipherable spiritual realm. As stewards of the land, we are being called to win back what has been lost, hidden or stolen.

We now turn our attention, therefore, to the subject of *the healing of land*.

Part 3

The Healing of Land

SEVEN

TAKING
RESPONSIBILITY

ealing the land is intimately connected with people. What people think, do and say has a direct bearing on either the extension of the Kingdom of God or the resistance of others to it. And the manner in which a steward looks after the property of the landowner has a direct bearing on the fruitfulness of his stewardship, as well as on the response of the landowner himself.

In the previous sections we have viewed various types of defilement on the land, and how these result in a foothold of sin that can affect both present and future generations. Such a foothold develops into a stronghold that affects the way people think and act, both individually and corporately, and releases a curse on the land.

Now let's view in greater detail how these strongholds can be cleansed from the land, thus setting people free and restoring God's intended fruitfulness for both land and people.

As we saw in the last chapter, Acts 16:4–5 tells us that the early Church grew in faith and numbers every day after she adopted the stewardship principles preached by the apostles and elders in Jerusalem. In keeping with the instruction of Numbers 35:33, we can see the importance of not allowing any defilement or spiritual pollution to have the right of entry to the land. When people take the correct responsibility for the sins and atrocities of previous generations (fallen steward-ship) that have resulted in defilement, the ongoing effect of those sins is ended, and reconciliation between the groups now living in these land areas can take place.

This process, called identificational repentance, is in keep-ing with Paul's imperative in 2 Corinthians 5:18–20 that through Christ we have "the ministry of reconciliation," and that we should be applying this message to our relationships with God and one another. When identificational repentance takes place, the unique giftings (which John Dawson refers to as "redemptive gifts") of the people living in these areas are re-leased and revealed. God's work among His people is no longer limited or inhibited because of their sin.

We will now see how confession, repentance, renouncing, deliverance and identificational repentance are all essential el-ements in implementing the healing of land.

First, two Old Testament examples of facing up to sin.

A Tale of Two Kings

The Old Testament offers numerous examples of the effects of sin in the lives of God's people. In many cases the leaders were as guilty as everyone else. But two kings of Judah ad-dressed the issue of sin without self-justification.

In 1 Kings we are given the account of Asa, who "did what was right in the eyes of the LORD, as his father David had done" (1 Kings 15:11). Asa expelled the male shrine prostitutes from Judah and removed the idols placed there by his ancestors. Verse 13 describes in detail how "he even deposed his grandmother Maacah from her position as queen mother, because she had made a repulsive Asherah pole." Asa was aware of the ramifications of idolatry and immorality on the land.

Verse 14 says that "although he did not remove the high places, Asa's heart was fully committed to the LORD all his life." Asa began the process of cleansing defilement from the land but did not go far enough. Still, as a leader of God's people, he modeled an important practice.

Second Kings 23 describes a more intensive undertaking of cleansing on the part of a later king of Judah. The reforms of Josiah, after finding the long-forgotten book of the law in the Temple, are some of the earliest examples of spiritual warfare and land cleansing in the Bible. He addressed each of the four defilements—idolatry, immorality, bloodshed and broken covenants. After he read and reaffirmed the words of the covenant to follow the Lord, "all the people" followed his example and pledged themselves to the requirements of God's covenant (see verse 3).

Josiah ordered the priests to remove all idolatrous articles from the Temple and to burn them. He dismissed the pagan priests who burned incense to Baal and to heavenly bodies. He removed the Asherah pole from the Temple and had it destroyed. He tore down the residences of the male shrine prostitutes and desecrated all the high places (idolatrous sites). All sacrifice to foreign gods was stopped, and any defilement, either on or beneath the ground, was promptly removed and destroyed.

Second Kings 23:25 gives this testimony of Josiah: "Neither before nor after Josiah was there a king like him who turned to the LORD as he did—with all his heart and with all his soul and with all his strength, in accordance with all the Law of Moses."

In his commitment to God, King Josiah recognized the necessity of removing and destroying whatever activity had been performed on the land that made God angry. Yet God's wrath continued because of the sin of Josiah's grandfather, Manasseh (see verse 26), who, like Josiah's father, Amon, had committed so many idolatrous abominations that God had vowed to "hand [Judah] over to their enemies" (2 Kings 21:14).

Concerning Josiah's actions, Robert Linthicum quotes Eugene H. Peterson:

> Here is Josiah, disgusted with the evil of his father and grandfather and determined to do something about it, but not knowing quite how. He had no blueprint, no direction, no counsel. The only thing he had inherited from his father and grandfather was fifty-seven years of evil. Now he had this powerful document about the love of God and our worship of Him (the Book of Deuteronomy), clear definitions of what is right and wrong, and explicit directions on how to make moral decisions and conduct intelligent worship.[1]

God could not bless or protect Israel, however, as Linthicum explains, if she did not wholeheartedly follow the Mosaic covenant. In addition, while the radical reform of Judah set in motion by Josiah seems laudable, "such reforms were only skin deep."[2] Linthicum points out that Jeremiah the prophet challenged the reform efforts of Josiah as shallow (see Jeremiah 6:16–21), and that true reform requires social justice and personal repentance, not just external actions devoid of a heartfelt response. Liturgical reform, in other words, is simply not enough. Listen to Jeremiah 7:5–7:

> "If you really change your ways and your actions and deal with each other justly, if you do not oppress the alien, the fatherless or the widow and do not shed innocent blood in this place, and if you do not follow other gods to your own harm, then I will let you live in this place . . . in the land . . . for ever and ever."

Regardless of the depth of their efforts, both Asa and Josiah demonstrate the necessity of responding to the holiness of God on both a corporate and personal level.

Any sin, whether individual or corporate, is an affront to the nature and character of God, and its effects always include the following:

- Feelings of guilt and shame
- Blaming others (moral cowardice)
- Reactionary sin in others (for example, anger or hate)
- Fear and mistrust in our own lives
- A desire to hide from God
- God's judgment
- Spiritual death
- A foothold for demonic activity and accusation
- Fodder for bondages and strongholds

Recall God's warning to Cain: "If you do what is right, will you not be accepted? But if you do not do what is right, sin is crouching at your door; it desires to have you, but you must master it" (Genesis 4:7).

It is important, taking all this into account, that we now examine the means by which people, churches, cities and lands can receive healing and deliverance. This is the good news God wants us to appropriate at every level of life!

Holiness and Cleansing

Few Christians would argue the point that we inherited original sin from our foreparents, Adam and Eve. Repeatedly we find God reminding us of our calling—who we are as stewards, what we should do, what we should not do, whom not to marry, what not to possess from earlier generations. His words "Be holy, because I am holy" (Leviticus 11:44) are repeated in many ways throughout the Bible.

Leviticus 20:22–24 refers to the new land into which God would bring His people, but warns them not to walk in the pestilence of its earlier inhabitants. Joshua 24:14–15, as we have seen, challenges God's people to choose whether to serve the gods their forefathers served in Egypt, or the gods of the Amorites, whose land they were now possessing, or the Lord. In Colossians 3 Paul reminds the Christians of their identity in Christ and tells them to recall what was put to death in their old nature, so as to reaffirm what should be established in their new nature in Christ. Old habits die hard, and Paul is giving us timely warning not to revert to the former ways of a fallen lifestyle.

Why is the issue of holiness on the part of His people so important to God? Deuteronomy 7:6 offers an insightful summary:

> For you are a people holy to the LORD your God. The LORD your God has chosen you out of all the peoples on the face of the earth to be his people, his treasured possession.

God is a jealous God and forbids our worshiping anyone or anything else (see Deuteronomy 5:7–9). God is also "jealous for his land" (Joel 2:18) and will permit no form of unholiness to reside in the lives of His people (see 1 Peter 2:9–10). God views sin seriously. He allows no justification for sin at any time.

Removing What Is Unholy

When King Saul was ordered to destroy the Amalekites and all their possessions (see 1 Samuel 15:3), he spared the Amalekite king and the best of the animals. The rest of the chapter unfolds Saul's self-justifying reasoning to Samuel. (We looked at this reasoning in chapter 5.) But as far as God was concerned, Saul had "rejected the word of the LORD" (verse 23), and God rejected him as king.

Why destroy the Amalekites and all their possessions? Because an *unholy virus* had to be prevented from attaching itself to God's people, and retaining any of the spoil of the Amalekites would result in defilement.

In the Old Testament, people, possessions and land were often destroyed if defilement and disobedience to God had occurred. Even a seemingly harmless artifact used for unholy purposes (these are termed "devoted things" in Joshua 7:15, referring to the object of Achan's sin) could become a fatal trap for His people.

Many times I have found such "devoted things" (for example, amulets, prayer beads or tourism mementos, such as dolls fashioned after Buddhist deities) in people's homes that had been used in earlier days for idolatrous purposes. The effect of having such objects in the household was deadly—causing such problems as marriage friction, constant sickness, oppression and despair—until they were removed and, in many cases, destroyed. The bottom line question I always ask people concerning a questionable item in their possession is this: "Does it bring honor and glory to God?" If not, why keep it?

In the New Testament the blood of Christ delivers mankind from the sin of defilement, and cleanses us as well as our areas of stewardship. We still have to maintain holy and healthy responsibility in our day-to-day stewardship of life. We live in a fallen world, after all, with enticing attractions that often camouflage danger for the Christian. Unlike Saul, we must be honest about our sin in order for it to be cleansed and removed (see 1 John 1:8–9). And such honesty needs to include the removal or destruction of anything that might have an unholy effect on God's people, as illustrated above.

This was a clearly defined New Testament principle (see Acts 19:18–20). We neglect to our detriment the profound words declared by a holy God in Deuteronomy 7:26: "Do not bring a detestable thing into your house or you, like it, will be set apart for destruction. Utterly abhor and detest it, for it is set apart for destruction." In a New Testament setting, we see this as God calling us to be responsible and holy in what we possess, in order that we not give an open door to spiritual invasion

177

or contamination. We must remember that we are relating to God, who has a clear biblical worldview on life!

These words from Deuteronomy are relevant for every generation that ever lived on the face of the earth. We have to be honest before the Lord, individually and corporately, and let Him reveal to us what we may hold as being precious but what He sees as being unholy.

The process of cleansing, therefore, is removing what is unholy in God's sight, which either limits or prevents His work and presence in our lives. Unholiness is the avenue through which the accuser of the brethren is given access to people and land. We may be in Christ, but if there are still entry points attached to us, we are vulnerable to demonic oppression.

A Closer Look at 2 Chronicles 7:14

Our personal stewardship, and our stewardship of our possessions and land, must be consistent at all times with the holiness of God. We must understand this in the context of a well-known verse:

> If my people, who are called by my name, will humble themselves and pray and seek my face and turn from their wicked ways, then will I hear from heaven and will forgive their sin and will heal their land.
>
> 2 Chronicles 7:14

We have seen that generational sin, or sin in the present, has a significant effect on the land. It can also affect the people who live on the land for generations to come. As people and their stewardship are redeemed, this in turn affects the land around them.

Redemption requires the confession of sins by the appropriate people and then the breaking of associated bondages (distorted relationships with God), with each other and with society as a whole. Demons can then be cast out in the name of Jesus, and words of healing spoken into the land. Second Chronicles 7:15 suggests a further blessing from God: "Now my eyes will be open and my ears attentive to the prayers offered in this place."

Let's take a look at the widely quoted requirements and promises of this previous verse.

What is the significance of being called by God's name? It is tied in, once again, with His holiness. We learn in the first few chapters of 2 Chronicles that Solomon was determined "to build a temple for the Name of the LORD" (2 Chronicles 2:1). God's name constitutes His character and nature—including His holiness.

In Solomon's dedication of the Temple, he asked this question: "But will God really dwell on earth with men?" (2 Chronicles 6:18). Solomon was acutely aware of the need for holiness when in the presence of God, and his entire prayer of dedication suggests the need for holiness in the lives of God's people, if they expect His presence to dwell in their midst. Second Chronicles 6:36–39 outlines the necessity of confession and repentance if we are to experience His forgiveness and presence.

Second Chronicles 7:14 makes this clear as well. God states that He will forgive sin in the lives of His people and heal their land *when* they humble themselves and turn from wickedness. Once sin is removed, the enemy has no more foothold or jurisdiction, either in the lives of the people of God or on their land. Then, when sin is removed, we experience God's healing in our lives, both individually and corporately.

The word for *heal* in this passage is *rapha*, a word used by ancient physicians meaning "to heal, to mend, to repair or to make whole." Used of people, *rapha* means restoration to a place of wholeness. Yet here the word is used in relation to land. As people are healed and restored in their relationship with, and stewardship before, God, the land is subsequently healed as well.

We constitute the temple of God in a corporate sense and in our individual relationships with Him (see 1 Corinthians 3:16–17; 6:19–20). Healing land is intimately connected, therefore, with the healing of people in their relationships with each other and with God. The spirit and witness of 2 Chronicles 7:14 lie at the heart of much New Testament teaching, even though the actual wording is not found in a specific text.

Consecrate Yourselves

Such healed relationships are birthed and rooted in humility and honesty. As the psalmist put it, "If I had cherished sin in my heart, the Lord would not have listened" (Psalm 66:18). In order to undertake the healing of the land from God's perspective, there must be no iniquity or uncleanness in our attitudes or relationships. There must, rather, be consecration.

Prior to crossing the Jordan, Joshua instructed the people, "Consecrate yourselves, for tomorrow the LORD will do amazing things among you" (Joshua 3:5).

Unholiness could spoil this consecration. This was the reason Achan's sin had to be addressed following the battle of Jericho. Let's look at this verse in its entirety. God told Joshua:

> "Go, consecrate the people. Tell them, 'Consecrate yourselves in preparation for tomorrow; for this is what the LORD, the God of Israel says: That which is devoted is among you, O Israel. You cannot stand against your enemies until you remove it.'"

> Joshua 7:13

In their book *Heal Our Land* Jimmy and Carol Owens relate to this standard of consecration:

> God is out to purify the Church—one of us at a time. He is after our characters. He is after our relationships with families,

friends, sweethearts, and business associates. All He needs from us are willing hearts. . . . Purity is the source of our credibility.[3]

Jimmy and Carol Owens see purity and humility as essential ingredients in the life of the Church if we are to consecrate ourselves for the healing of God's land. They refer to Numbers 16, a time when God was about to pour His judgment out on the people of Israel:

> Aaron the high priest runs into the midst of a rebellious congregation of Israel as God begins to pour out the discipline of death: "For there is wrath gone out from the LORD; the plague has begun!" (Numbers 16:46, AB). Holding a censer of fire and incense, a symbol of prayer, he makes atonement for them: "And he stood between the dead and the living, and the plague was stayed" (v. 48, AB). Just as it was part of Aaron's priestly duty, intercession is also a part of the church's duty as "priests unto God" (see Revelation 1:6; 5:10).[4]

The Owens also make reference to Daniel, pointing out that his prayers were effective because of the determination and humility in his posture (see Daniel 9:3). They observe "two principles . . . vital to the success of Daniel's intercession," principles corresponding to the two definitions offered by *Young's Bible Concordance* for the Hebrew word used for *pray* in 2 Chronicles 7:14. Here are the principles:

1. Daniel judged himself first. He confessed his own sins, not claiming any personal goodness but throwing himself on the goodness of God for deliverance.
2. He prayed habitually. Daniel didn't wait for days of desperation to sharpen up his prayer life; he was a prayer warrior with a disciplined spirit. And he persevered until he heard from heaven.[5]

Daniel prayed in this manner for the sins and the leadership of his nation.

181

Relationship, humility, purity, perseverance—all are essential ingredients as we consecrate ourselves to the task of standing in the gap, so that God's healing of the land can take place. Surely this is His intention for our land, for our cities, for ourselves.

The book of Ezekiel ends with these words: "The name of the city from that time on will be: THE LORD IS THERE." What a simple yet profound statement! When land is healed, God's presence dwells in the midst of His people. As He promised Solomon: "I have chosen and consecrated this temple so that my Name may be there forever. My eyes and my heart will always be there" (2 Chronicles 7:16).

Surely this is God's desire for every city.

Identificational Repentance

We have made several references to the term *identificational repentance*. It is important for us to understand this atoning action from God's perspective. We have already seen the underlying principle:

> "Do not pollute the land where you are. Bloodshed pollutes the land, and atonement cannot be made for the land on which blood has been shed, *except by the blood of the one who shed it.*"
>
> Numbers 35:33, emphasis added

A startling biblical example of identificational sacrifice— somewhat shocking to twentieth-century minds—is found in the story of Saul and the Gibeonites.

In Joshua 9 the Gibeonites tricked Joshua into making a treaty with them. Generations later King Saul broke that treaty by attempting to kill the Gibeonites (see 2 Samuel 21:2). Years later, during the reign of Saul's successor, the people experienced famine for three years. David sought the Lord to learn the reason, and 2 Samuel 21:1 records the Lord's response: "It is on account of Saul and his blood-stained house; it is because he put the Gibeonites to death."

David and the Israelites reaped the *consequences* of iniquity that had been sown in previous generations through David's predecessor. Even though the original treaty had come about by trickery, God still held later descendants responsible for honoring that covenant.

The land was cleansed only when seven of Saul's descendants were sacrificed before the Lord. Second Samuel 21:14 states categorically that "after that God answered prayer in behalf of the land."

Responsibility for Sin in the Old Testament

Ezra, Nehemiah and Daniel are often cited as prime examples of identificational repentance. Ponder part of the prayers of each of these righteous men:

> "O my God, I am too ashamed and disgraced to lift up my face to you, my God, because our sins are higher than our heads and our guilt has reached to the heavens. . . . For we have disregarded the commands you gave through your servants the prophets. . . . Here we are before you in our guilt, though because of it not one of us can stand in your presence."
>
> Ezra 9:6, 10–11, 15

Then Nehemiah:

> ". . . I confess the sins we Israelites, including myself and my father's house, have committed against you. We have acted very wickedly toward you. We have not obeyed the commands, decrees and laws you gave your servant Moses."
>
> Nehemiah 1:6–7

And Daniel:

> "We have sinned and done wrong. We have been wicked and have rebelled; we have turned away from your commands

183

and laws. We have not listened to your servants the prophets.
... Lord, you are righteous, but this day we are covered with
shame...."

Daniel 9:5–7

Each of these leaders, though not personally guilty of
wickedness, disobedience and rebellion, confessed these sins
on behalf of their people, both present and past.

Responsibility for Sin in the New Testament

The New Testament builds on the foundation of identificational repentance, acknowledging our responsibility for sins
we inherit as well as for sins we commit. Let's remember that
the New Testament Church was using the Old Testament as
its Bible, and the issue of praying on behalf of other people was
a known and accepted practice.

Jesus Himself addressed the issue of guilt for past sins that
still had relevance for the present generation:

> "Woe to you, teachers of the law and Pharisees, you hyp-
> ocrites! You build tombs for the prophets and decorate the
> graves of the righteous. And you say, 'If we had lived in the
> days of our forefathers, we would not have taken part with
> them in shedding the blood of the prophets.'"

Matthew 23:29–30

Then Jesus predicted that the Pharisees and teachers of the
law would do just as their forefathers had done:

> "Therefore I am sending you prophets and wise men and
> teachers. Some of them you will kill and crucify; others you
> will flog in your synagogues and pursue from town to town.
> And so upon you will come all the righteous blood that has
> been shed on earth, from the blood of righteous Abel to the
> blood of Zechariah son of Berekiah, whom you murdered be-

184

tween the temple and the altar. I tell you the truth, all this will come upon this generation."

verses 34–36

Notice that Jesus addresses the leaders as if they had committed that murder, even though He was describing the actions of their forefathers. In other words, guilt is borne and even reinforced by successive generations!

When the deacon and evangelist Stephen made his defense before the Sanhedrin in the first years of the Church, he drew their attention to the sins of their forefathers and the consequences of those sins (see Acts 7:39–53). Again he was holding the people responsible for the sins of their forefathers—those who had killed the prophets announcing the coming of the Righteous One. They were doing now just as their forefathers had done, rejecting and ignoring the law and resisting the Holy Spirit (see verses 51–53). Same problem, same sin, same responsibility!

When one generation decides to stand in the gap, accept the consequences of the sins of previous generations and appropriate the shed blood of Christ, an end will come to the inherited curse, as well as to the consequences of that curse. Only the cross can finally remove the guilt placed on mankind. Galatians 3:13 explains that Jesus became a curse on our behalf by identifying with our sin and taking the penalty of our sins on Himself—the ultimate identification with sin.

What about Ezekiel 18?

This passage (which needs to be read in its entirety) is often used by opponents of identificational repentance as evidence that we do not have to stand in the gap and repent on behalf of the sins of earlier generations. A few highlights from that chapter:

The word of the LORD came to me: "What do you people mean by quoting this proverb about the land of Israel: 'The fathers eat sour grapes, and the children's teeth are set on edge'?

185

As surely as I live, declares the Sovereign LORD, you will no longer quote this proverb in Israel.... The soul who sins is the one who will die. . . . The son will not share the guilt of the father, nor will the father share the guilt of the son."

verses 1–4, 20

So far as this passage is concerned, it is true that nobody can die for the sins of another person. But the *consequences* of generational sin—a stewardship issue—can still influence the person and his life, even his nation. It is the *consequence* that is not removed and that must be confessed in order for a foothold to be removed from that lineage.

Opponents may ask, Hasn't generational sin been dealt with under the New Covenant with the shedding of Christ's blood? Again, it a matter of understanding the consequences of sin from God's perspective. Let's look at two New Testament examples.

First, in John 9, we read of Jesus healing the man born blind. On that occasion the disciples were expressing the biblical worldview, which Jesus did not negate. In other words, it *could* have been either the man's personal sin or the sin of his parents that had caused his blindness. Jesus did not close the door on generational sin as a potential cause of affliction. But He said simply, "Neither this man nor his parents sinned . . . but this happened so that the work of God might be displayed in his life" (verse 3).

Second, in the book of Acts we read about Simon the Sorcerer, who became a believer and was baptized—yet this did not break the bondage over him of his own bitterness and the sin that obviously still had an influence on his life, in spite of his conversion. He was "full of bitterness and captive to sin" (Acts 8:23). This passage indicates that even Christians may need to be delivered from spiritual oppression that is the consequence of inherited sin. At times this is apparent only when one becomes a Christian, at which time the hidden agendas of inherited stewardship are suddenly exposed, requiring specific ministry.

Romans 3:23 makes it clear that "all have sinned and fall short of the glory of God." So we are able to identify with the roots of any sin on the land, even though we may not have been directly involved with that sin ourselves. At times, however, effective repentance requires our more specific participation, if the sin involves issues in the past connected with our family, culture or office (for example, pastor, mayor, police chief, president).

Isn't it remarkable that Nehemiah and Ezra, both righteous men, did not hesitate to identify with the sins of their nation? John Dawson, noting this, observes that "the unredeemed cannot make atonement for the land. The pagan cannot go up into the gap and present the blood of the Lamb. This is the privilege and responsibility of God's people, even if they are just a remnant in the land."[6] Dawson adds that "the act of confession is as powerful in effecting the cleansing and healing of nations as it is in individuals."[7]

The Christian is responsible to apply the blood of the Lamb to any form of iniquity that has taken place on the land. When this is done from a position of humility, God hears from heaven, forgives our sin and heals our land. God is indeed a heart reader, not a lip reader!

Confession and Forgiveness

The confession of sin releases the immediacy of God's forgiveness over the activities that have separated us from His presence. Recall Nehemiah's prayer: "I *confess* the sins we Israelites, including myself and my father's house, have committed against you. We have acted very wickedly toward you" (Nehemiah 1:6–7, emphasis added).

187

First John 1:8–9 explains the principle:"If we claim to be without sin, we deceive ourselves and the truth is not in us. If we *confess* our sins, he is faithful and just and will forgive us our sins and purify us from all unrighteousness" (emphasis added). James 5:16 puts it this way:"*Confess* your sins to each other and pray for each other so that you may be healed. The prayer of a righteous man is powerful and effective" (emphasis added).

In seeking forgiveness, we are doing the following:

- Admitting the true nature of the sin, with no justification
- "Owning" the sin and resolving to turn from it
- Forgiving everyone involved in the origins of that sin (the roots)
- Accepting the forgiveness promised in God's Word
- Being willing to forgive ourselves
- Renouncing the negative characteristics of that sin affecting the individual or the community
- Choosing the way of righteousness

In recognizing the power of our confession before God, whether for our own sin or on behalf of others, we are availing ourselves of God's forgiveness.

Breaking Bondages

Having grown in our understanding of holiness, consecration, identificational repentance, confession and forgiveness, we are in a position to deal with the final step in this process of healing the land: breaking the bondages and barriers that have separated us from God's love and healing. This principle extends from the individual right through to an entire nation. We need to recall that bondages (distorted relationships) are the result of sin that has opened the door to demonic activity.

At this point we need to understand the ministry of binding and loosing:

> "I tell you the truth, whatever you bind on earth will be bound in heaven, and whatever you loose on earth will be loosed in heaven. Again, I tell you that if two of you on earth agree about anything you ask for, it will be done for you by my Father in heaven."
>
> Matthew 18:18–19

In his book *Overcoming the Dominion of Darkness,* Gary D. Kinnaman gives a theological perspective on binding and loosing:

> The use of the phrase *binding and loosing* did not, in fact, originate with Jesus. It was a frequent expression of first-century Jewish rabbinical dialect. According to Alexander Bruce in *The Expositor's Greek New Testament*, to bind and loose (Greek: *deo* and *luo*) meant simply "to prohibit and to permit," that is, to establish rules (Vol. 1, p. 225). The Jewish religious authorities at the time of Christ retained the right to establish guidelines for, or keys to, religious practice and social interaction.
>
> But *deo* (to bind, tie) also expresses supernatural control. In Luke 13:15–16, Jesus rebuked a Jewish leader, "You hypocrites! Doesn't each of you on the Sabbath untie [Greek: *luo,* loose] his ox or donkey from the stall and lead it out to give it water? Then should not this woman, a daughter of Abraham, whom Satan has kept bound [Greek: *deo,* bind], for eighteen long years, be set free [Greek: *luo,* loose] on the Sabbath day from what bound her?"
>
> Binding and loosing is an activity of spiritual warfare.[8]

There is a supernatural aspect of binding and loosing going on in the spiritual realm in concert with what we are doing in the physical realm. Cindy Jacobs summarizes the ministry of binding and loosing:

Binding stops the enemy's attacks. Loosing releases or permits God's will to enter the situation because God has willed that His purposes be carried out by asking in prayer.[9]

Whether we are praying for individuals or for a corporate community, binding the work of the enemy follows confession, repentance and forgiveness of sin. In this way the bondages and strongholds are addressed directly, evil spirits that may have had the right of access to that situation are cast out, and God's healing and authority in that situation are loosed.

To summarize, we are effectively appropriating the atoning work of Christ into the situation at hand. This involves following scriptural guidelines for the confession and forgiveness of sins, the breaking of bondages, the removal of evil spirits, and the speaking forth of God's healing into the wounds that have affected either the person or the community.

Using Elements in Spiritual Cleansing

At times God may also require certain symbolic acts when He knows that an issue in the spiritual realm must be addressed in a specific manner.

Over the many years I have been involved in the ministry of cleansing and healing the land, there have been times that it was appropriate, for spiritual cleansing in a prophetic and sacramental manner, to utilize the elements of salt, water, oil or holy Communion, recognizing that at times spiritual cleansing may also involve physical cleansing and the removal of specific objects.

The Use of Salt

At times our ministry teams have found that prayers of confession, forgiveness, deliverance and healing are not adequate to deal with certain spiritual issues. This is often the case when sin has had a foothold over several generations, and when a demonic grip on a territory seems to be affecting areas of community life like churches, businesses, politics or schools. It is also the case when a place of ministry is located on a former massacre site or place of worship where some form of bloodshed has taken place.

At such times we use consecrated salt, undertaking a prophetic act on a symbolic basis that has an effect in the spiritual realm. (We will get an idea in our discussion of water how this might be done.)

Salt is a cleansing agent. It is also a substance that releases flavor, as you quickly appreciate when you are making Scottish porridge. The flavor of the porridge oats is slowly and wonderfully released through the work of the salt!

Salt symbolizes in the physical realm an activity or action taking place in the spiritual realm. For example, 2 Kings 2:19–22 shows the symbolic use of salt in removing the impurity from defiled water. It is interesting that Scripture refers to the healing of water, since that implies the displacement of something unholy:

> The men of the city said to Elisha, "Look, our lord, this town is well situated, as you can see, but the water is bad and the land is unproductive."
>
> "Bring me a new bowl," he said, "and put salt in it." So they brought it to him.
>
> Then he went out to the spring and threw the salt into it, saying, "This is what the LORD says: 'I have healed this water. Never again will it cause death or make the land unproductive.'" And the water has remained wholesome to this day, according to the word Elisha had spoken.

Salt was added to the water to address this issue of defilement. It reversed the effect of sin on the land, which was unproductive, and released the water to its original purpose.

The use of salt is key in understanding biblical covenants among Bible people. A ceremony or ritual could be confirmed or ratified with salt. Salt symbolizes faith and loyalty. God commanded that "every offering of your grain offering you shall season with salt; you shall not allow the salt of the covenant of your God to be lacking from your grain offering. With all your offerings you shall offer salt" (Leviticus 2:13, NKJV).

Numbers 18:19 mentions "an everlasting covenant of salt before the LORD for both you and your offspring." *The Spirit-Filled Life Bible* notes that "the covenant of salt probably refers to the salt eaten in the solemnizing of a contract. It attests the permanence of the agreement."[10]

In chapter 3 we examined some of the significant practices and issues involved in covenant-making between individuals. At times in ancient Israel, when two people made a pact or covenant, they took a pinch of salt out of a little salt pouch worn on their waists and placed each pinch into the bag of the other party involved in the agreement. This indicated the intimacy and sharing of the agreement.

Ezekiel 43:23–24 commands that "you shall offer a young bull without blemish, and a ram from the flock without blemish. When you offer them before the LORD, the priests shall throw salt on them, and they will offer them up as a burnt offering to the LORD" (NKJV).

In the New Testament we find that salt preserves people from corruption. In Matthew 5:13 Jesus declared, "You are the salt of the earth. But if the salt loses its saltiness, how can it be made salty again? It is no longer good for anything, except to be thrown out and trampled by men."

God wants us to be salt on earth for the purpose of cleansing, as well as for incarnating the reality of what lies hidden in the spiritual realm. Paul says in Colossians 4:6, "Let your conversation be always full of grace, seasoned with salt, so that you may know how to answer everyone."

As we view these references to salt in the Bible, we find that it is a symbol of incorruptibility; that it preserves people from corruption; that it can be a form of judgment on people and land; that it is a sign of covenant and agreement; and that it symbolizes endurance and perseverance on the part of God's people.

The Use of Water

Scripture has much to say concerning the symbol of water. Here is part of the conversation between Jesus and the woman at the well:

> The Samaritan woman said to him, "You are a Jew and I am a Samaritan woman. How can you ask me for a drink?" (For Jews do not associate with Samaritans.)
>
> Jesus answered her, "If you knew the gift of God and who it is that asks you for a drink, you would have asked him and he would have given you living water. . . . Whoever drinks the water I give him will never thirst. Indeed, the water I give him will become in him a spring of water welling up to eternal life."
>
> John 4:9–10, 14

Water in this sense brings refreshment and relief from thirst. It is continual refreshing in the Person of Christ and the power of the Holy Spirit. Water used in the sacrament of baptism indicates the removal of sin and the rising again in new life in Christ.

Like salt, water serves to bring definition to life. It represents the removal of defilement, the sense of being washed clean, having a thirst for life that is fully satisfied. Water and salt are both used to deal with sin and (as we have seen in 2 Kings 2) to reverse the effect of sin on the land.

There is nothing magical in salt or water. But when used in the power of the Holy Spirit, by His direction, they release the integrity of the Lord into situations so as to remove sin and defilement in the spiritual, and then physical, realm. There is a deep connection here with the redemptive nature of Jesus Christ.

As an Anglican clergyman I have used holy water for many years in a variety of ministries, particularly in connection with healing and deliverance. With salt symbolizing the removal of corruption, and water symbolizing the living reservoir of God's grace, their combination can be a symbolic act of significant authority in both the spiritual and physical realms.

Often I mix the salt and water together while reading such Scripture as Psalm 118, John 5:25–29, 1 Corinthians 15:51–57 and Hebrews 9:11–22. I am making a declaration into the spiritual realm, proclaiming that through the use of these elements, what is unholy can be cleansed—made holy and set aside for God's purposes.

Salt and water also symbolize the faithful prayers of the servants of God acting on His behalf to remove the defilement that has brought judgment on the land. The combination of salt and water is blessed accordingly for the purpose at hand. Then leaders and intercessors sprinkle the water sparingly, asking God to reveal the depth of the issues at hand. At times they may offer a prayer such as this:

> Father, as we sprinkle this water in Your holy name, deliver this place, deliver this room, deliver this land from all evil spirits, all vain imaginations and phantasm, projections of all deceits of the evil one. Bind and bid them from harming or affecting anyone or anything as they depart to the place appointed for them by Jesus, there to remain for ever, so that the incarnate God who came to give peace can bring peace. Amen.

Sometimes, confronted by entrenched demonic defilement, leaders and intercessors pray into the very roots of a property. They may address the very words of a contract or covenant made by the original occupiers of the land that was contrary to God's plan. When there is entrenched defilement on the land, they may use a prayer like this:

> In the name of God the Trinity, Father, Son and Holy Spirit, by the power of the cross and the blood of the Lord Jesus Christ, we bind the spirits, powers, forces of the earth, the underground,

the air, the water, the fire, the netherworld and the satanic forces of nature. We rebuke any curses, hexes or spells and send them back to where they came from, to the place appointed for them by Jesus. We bind all demonic interplay, interaction and communication. We claim the protection of the shed blood of Jesus Christ over [name of person or building or place]. Amen.

As I suggested earlier, while we can all be involved in praying through issues of sin that have taken place on the land, since "all have sinned and fall short of the glory of God," it is nonetheless beneficial to have representatives of the area pray this prayer, particularly when identificational repentance is being undertaken. It is important that local leaders and intercessors be involved in this kind of prayer ministry together, listening to the direction of the Holy Spirit, to retain balance and integrity at all times.

The Use of Anointing Oil

Here is the original recipe for anointing oil:

> Then the LORD said to Moses, "Take the following fine spices: 500 shekels of liquid myrrh, half as much (that is, 250 shekels) of fragrant cinnamon, 250 shekels of fragrant cane, 500 shekels of cassia—all according to the sanctuary shekel—and a hin of olive oil. Make these into a sacred anointing oil, a fragrant blend, the work of a perfumer. It will be the sacred anointing oil. . . . Say to the Israelites, 'This is to be my sacred anointing oil for the generations to come. Do not pour it on men's bodies and do not make any oil with the same formula. It is sacred, and you are to consider it sacred. Whoever makes perfume like it and whoever puts it on anyone other than a priest must be cut off from his people.'"
>
> Exodus 30:22–25, 31–33

Some will argue that the recipe for holy oil in this fascinating passage was exclusively for the use of the priests during Old Testament times. For example:

Samuel took the horn of oil and anointed [David] in the presence of his brothers, and from that day on the Spirit of the LORD came upon David in power.

1 Samuel 16:13

Yet 1 Peter 2:9 reminds us that *we* are "a chosen people, a royal priesthood, a holy nation, a people belonging to God." Passages such as the instructions for preparing anointing oil are really addressing the subject of holiness. People, places, sanctuaries—everything involved in the worship of the holy, living God is to be holy. Even under the New Covenant, we are still required to maintain our relationship with God as His holy undefiled servants, stewards of all He has entrusted to us.

The issue of anointing oil, therefore, is still a holy, powerful ministry of, and to, the people of God, simply because we *are* a chosen people and a royal priesthood. At times God has instructed our prayer teams to prepare oil in the way outlined in Exodus 30, and at other times simply to use olive oil and then bless it for the purpose at hand, in the name of the Lord.

The use of anointing oil under the direction of the Holy Spirit releases the power of God in areas of healing and restoration, as well as for the release of faith and forgiveness:

Is any one of you sick? He should call the elders of the church to pray over him and anoint him with oil in the name of the Lord. And the prayer offered in faith will make the sick person well; the Lord will raise him up. If he has sinned, he will be forgiven.

James 5:14–15

In Hebrews 1:9 oil is used for the release of joy:

"You have loved righteousness and hated wickedness; therefore God, your God, has set you above your companions by anointing you with the oil of joy."

A cross reference to Isaiah 61:3 shows the people of God being given "a crown of beauty instead of ashes, the oil of gladness instead of mourning." A "reverse" takes place when holy oil is used under the direction and authority of the Lord. Indeed, this is holiness—being set aside for God's purposes. And here is the psalmist quoted in Hebrews:

> You love righteousness and hate wickedness; therefore God, your God, has set you above your companions by anointing you with the oil of joy. All your robes are fragrant with myrrh and aloes and cassia; from palaces adorned with ivory the music of the strings makes you glad.
>
> Psalm 45:8

David's reference to anointing with oil is well-known:

> You prepare a table before me in the presence of my enemies. You anoint my head with oil; my cup overflows.
>
> Psalm 23:5

Again we get a sense of the extravagance of God coming on and within the lives of His people—restoring, empowering, releasing, healing and establishing the sense of identity between a loving Father and His child. This must be what David experienced when he was anointed by Samuel.

Finally these words in Psalm 133 connect oil with the issue of unity:

> How good and pleasant it is when brothers live together in unity! It is like precious oil poured on the head, running down on the beard, running down on Aaron's beard, down upon the collar of his robes.
>
> Psalm 133:1–2

In all these Scriptures we see oil used for appropriating the Kingdom of God within the lives of His people. The process involves God's presence, His release of power, His sense of unity,

His forgiveness of our sins and the establishment of our identities in Christ as children of God, servants and much more.

Oil is used in a symbolic way with prayer as a means of establishing God's authority over a person's life or over a geographical area. We use it to reveal the *topos*—the foothold of sin that has caused defilement. Oil establishes the mark of God's authority and sovereignty. So it is that we literally anoint buildings, doorways, windows—indeed, the parameters of the ground associated with the people and places requiring liberation.

It is important to emphasize once again that this activity is symbolic and not magical. The oil represents something specific taking place in the spiritual realm; it involves revelation, release and restoration.

Holy Communion

Whether we call this the breaking of bread, the Lord's Supper, the Eucharist, holy Communion or Mass, we are referring to the other major sacrament in the Christian Church, alongside holy baptism. I have found it important to participate in Communion in areas where unholy sacrifice or defilement has taken place.

The blood shed by Jesus Christ is very precious in the sight of God. Leviticus 17:11 says that "the life of a creature is in the blood, and I have given it to you to make atonement for yourselves on the altar; it is the blood that makes atonement for one's life." This is why Old Testament sacrifices were so important. The blood was used for the purpose of cleansing—covering for our sin.

The Communion table reminds us of the precious, atoning blood of Christ. It is important to acknowledge the teaching of Hebrews:

> When Christ came as high priest of the good things that are already here, he went through the greater and more per-

fect tabernacle that is not man-made, that is to say, not a part
of this creation. He did not enter by means of the blood of
goats and calves; but he entered the Most Holy Place once for
all by his own blood, having obtained eternal redemption. The
blood of goats and bulls and the ashes of a heifer sprinkled on
those who are ceremonially unclean sanctify them so that they
are outwardly clean. How much more, then, will the blood of
Christ, who through the eternal Spirit offered himself un-
blemished to God, cleanse our consciences from acts that lead
to death, so that we may serve the living God!

Hebrews 9:11–14

Verse 22 makes this interesting point regarding the Old Testament covenant: "The law requires that nearly everything be
cleansed with blood, and without the shedding of blood there
is no forgiveness." But blood has been shed. Christ "has appeared once for all at the end of the ages to do away with sin
by the sacrifice of himself" (verse 26). The blood of Jesus Christ
cleanses us from sin.

We are finding that when we celebrate Communion together on the land where sin has taken place, we are undertaking a prophetic act that bears witness in the spiritual realm.
Whatever is blemished, whatever is defiled, is being brought
before the Lord by His servants so that the cleansing blood of
Christ becomes the final sacrifice required for the removal of
sin in that area. This reveals the depth of meaning behind Numbers 35:33, which I will quote here again in full since it emphasizes the importance of what Christ has done for us in this
regard:

> "Do not pollute the land where you are. Bloodshed pol-
> lutes the land, and atonement cannot be made for the land on
> which blood has been shed, *except by the blood of the one who
> shed it.*"

emphasis added

Remember that the consequence of sin on the land is serious from God's perspective; the land is "punished . . . for its sin" (Leviticus 18:25). But by the act of celebrating the Lord's Supper, we appropriate by faith the shed blood of Christ on that land—which is owned by God—in order to expiate the iniquity and blemish of sin in that place.

It is good, whenever possible, to have representatives of the original inhabitants of the land join together for confession, repentance, renunciation, breaking bondages and healing wounds. It is also good to try to ensure that those who have been offended or trespassed against are ministered to by those who have done the offending. As we share Communion, we are acknowledging the power of the blood of Christ in the cleansing of His land. We are also acting as responsible stewards of His property by releasing the promises and blessings of God on His people and land.

The Seven Blessings of God on the Land

Leviticus 26:4–10 presents seven categories of blessings that God longs to bestow on His people when they live and walk and work in obedience to Him:

- *Ecological health:* "I will send you rain in its season, and the ground will yield its crops and the trees of the field their fruit" (verse 4).
- *Economic health:* "Your threshing will continue until grape harvest and the grape harvest will continue until planting, and you will eat all the food you want and live in safety in your land" (verse 5).
- *Personal security:* "I will grant peace in the land, and you will lie down and no one will make you afraid" (verse 6a).

- *Civil security:* "I will remove savage beasts from the land, and the sword will not pass through your country" (verse 6b).
- *International security:* "You will pursue your enemies, and they will fall by the sword before you. Five of you will chase a hundred, and a hundred of you will chase ten thousand" (verses 7–8a).
- *Honor and growth:* "I will look on you with favor and make you fruitful and increase your numbers, and I will keep my covenant with you" (verse 9).
- *Innovation and creativity:* "You will still be eating last year's harvest when you will have to move it out to make room for the new" (verse 10).

God gives further promises to His people for their obedience:

> "I will put my dwelling place among you, and I will not abhor you. I will walk among you and be your God, and you will be my people. I am the LORD your God, who brought you out of Egypt so that you would no longer be slaves to the Egyptians; I broke the bars of your yoke and enabled you to walk with heads held high."
>
> verses 11–13

These blessings could also be termed the seven transformation principles that are being witnessed in our day around the world. As communities of all sizes are cleansed of their sin and fallen stewardship, these transformation principles are being displayed in their social, political, economic and spiritual aspects.

If we were to investigate each of these seven categories in detail, we would find, across the globe, an exciting development in concert with God's promise of blessing, fueled by the aggressive prayers of a mobilized Church. God needs to have

201

His people actively involved in the removal of whatever issues impede transformation. Once these are gone, His blessings are released. We are now seeing this taking place in actual communities of various shapes and sizes.

In terms of *ecological health*, in communities that have begun to experience such change, there is a distinct improvement in natural resources, while climatic conditions have actually become more conducive to agriculture, resulting in higher productivity from the land. Consider Almolonga, Guatemala, utterly transformed spiritually, which now enjoys as many as three productive harvests a year, and which is known for its carrots as large as a person's forearm!

Regarding *economic health*, transformed communities can expect a higher export potential, a better return on investment, a heightened degree of prudence in business and management, and increasing strength in worldwide economics. Kiambu, Kenya, is one such community that has begun to experience economic change accompanying the change in spiritual climate.

Heightened *personal security* includes lower crime rates and less fearful communities. Changes also include the removal of unrest (see Psalm 144:14) and fewer disputes within families and marriages. In other words, the home becomes a place of greater security. This is also the experience of Kiambu. Its high crime rate dropped, Kiambu is now a place of low crime and personal safety. The same is recorded of towns in the days of the Finney revival and during the revival in the Scottish Hebrides in the early 1950s under Duncan Campbell. When people focus collectively on the Lord, the entire community atmosphere begins to change.

In terms of *civil security*, certain communities are experiencing a decrease in business corruption, such as Cali, Colombia, with the removal of that city's ruling drug lords. When corporate respect for law and order increases, there appears to be greater protection over people's corporate life and work.

A pastor from a community of thirty thousand in northern British Columbia shared with me that since the local churches have begun praying and working together strategically, car theft has dropped from as many as thirty thefts in a month to sometimes as few as one. Again, this is in keeping with a praying, united Church seeking transformation for the community.

Regarding *international security*, a greater sense of God's destiny and presence and direction will permeate the nation, along with the removal of the fear of untimely war and persecution. Although Canada still has much ground to cover in this regard, the nation as a whole has a definite sense of security and safety in comparison to many other nations. Several prayer movements now exist in this land, many of them hearing a deeper sense of God's call on Canada as a nation of reconciliation and healing for other nations. Local prayer initiatives spawn larger movements, which at times address national issues. In the summer of 1999, for example, a large gathering of church leaders and intercessors met together in Winnipeg to address the subject of Canada's treatment of the Jewish people. God is preparing this nation for a divine visitation, province by province and territory by territory.

In terms of *honor and growth*, certain locales are experiencing a sense of God's visitation and habitation. The reflection of His purpose and vision there tends to be strengthened. There is a greater sense of divine guidance and purpose over the land as a whole. Church leaders in Hemet, California, testify that their community is not the same today as in former years. The sociopolitical fabric has changed remarkably, in concert with the prayers and involvement of a united, praying Church. That city now has a new appreciation for God's people, as God has honored the prayers of His Church.

Finally, regarding *innovation and creativity*, formerly untapped riches, resources and creativity are being revealed on an individual and corporate basis. Such a nation enjoys increased provision for sharing its resources with other nations. It also has a heightened understanding of the stewardship of God's time, talent and treasure.

Singapore is an extraordinary city, island and nation, all in one small area of land. The diversity and economic strength of this nation far outweigh its geographical size, and its computer technology has influenced many parts of the world. Several leading churches in this city work and pray together for the transformation of their nation, and Dr. C. Peter Wagner testifies on the videotape *Love Singapore* (one of the prayer tools being used by the Singaporian Church) that she could become the first transformed nation.

Almolonga, Guatemala, which is enjoying a revitalized economy from its bountiful harvests, now attracts agrologists from various parts of the world to learn the secrets of its success. Even a small community such as Mgbarrakuma Village in southern Nigeria is experiencing change following its corporate decision to revoke a continuum of three hundred years of idol worship and to make a covenant with the living God. Word is spreading about a new clay substance found on the land that is highly profitable for pottery. Villagers are learning that the God they now worship is also the God who has ecology under His authority.

Whether to a community, a city or a nation, God longs to release His honor and blessing on His land and people, causing them to become a blessing and testimony to the rest of the world. "Blessed is the nation whose God is the LORD, the people he chose for his inheritance" (Psalm 33:12).

Stewards of Reconciliation

The term *act of God* is seen regularly as a small-print clause on insurance policies removing their responsibility to underwrite loss in times of natural disasters. In other words, God gets the blame!

An act of God is, in fact, a demonstration of His divine activity in the lives of His people. When we appropriate His principles of proper stewardship in bringing restoration to the land, the impact of heaven experienced on earth releases transformation.

A Christian mission organization asked if I would help the directors pray through some difficult issues they had inherited over a period of years. Previous directorship and management had become involved in immorality, excessive control and questionable accounting practices. As a result there was continual unrest and manipulation on the part of the employees, and constant corporate preoccupation with finances.

The ministry representatives with whom I prayed were honest, allowing for no justification or rationalization of sin. We addressed the roots and original vision of the founders, gave thanks to God for what was good and dealt with the issues of sin and bondage that had subtly crept into the ministry over the years. We prayed about various positions of responsibility within the ministry, since as each office had been vacated, the next person had fallen prey to the same problems. The fruit gave clear testimony to defiled roots!

Within a matter of days following our prayer, economic health, honor and growth, as well as new areas of divine security and creativity, all began to develop. Within days the largest single donation ever recorded in the history of the organization was received—a six-figure sum! On its heels came several smaller (four-figure!) checks. Certain employees who had been causing problems left, and a new sense of God's holiness and presence began to pervade the ministry.

The organization is now preparing for a new season of dynamic ministry. They have experienced an act of God—indeed the blessings of God on their "land."

Returning to our early look at the parable of the sower and the seed, I can bear witness that case studies are developing even as I write, showing the rocky places and thorns being removed from the land and the birds being kept at bay. Many in the Church are witnessing lands and peoples entering into a great experience of God's harvest in their lives.

In this chapter we have looked at some of the issues involved in healing land, so that the promise of 2 Chronicles 7:14 can be realized. We are, in effect, dealing with the issue of 2 Corinthians 4:3–4:

> Even if our gospel is veiled, it is veiled to those who are perishing. The god of this age has blinded the minds of unbelievers, so that they cannot see the light of the gospel of the glory of Christ, who is the image of God.

As Christ's ambassadors (see 2 Corinthians 5:18–20), we are the stewards of reconciliation between individuals, between individuals and God, and between corporate communities and God. As land is healed, the veil of blindness is lifted and the eyes of communities are opened to the Gospel. *It is possible to change the disposition of an entire community in its attitude toward God!* In fact, this is not only possible but required for effective evangelism with lasting results.

It is interesting to reflect on the fact that while it was in the Garden of Eden that mankind effectively defiled the land, thus removing the intimacy of God's life and presence in his midst, the resurrection of Jesus also took place in a garden. It was there that God's word of restoration for mankind could begin.

The fourth gospel adds an interesting insight not found in the synoptic gospels about the resurrection of Jesus. John 20:7 refers to the burial cloth that had been placed around the head of Jesus when His body was prepared for the tomb. We are told in this passage that, after the resurrection, "the cloth was folded up by itself, separate from the linen." In Old Testament days, when a Jewish carpenter completed a project for a customer, he would take a cloth, fold it up and hand it to the customer. It was his way of saying, "The job has been completed in full."

The work of the Son of God for the redemption and trans-formation of mankind was completed with His resurrection. The principles of transformation for the individual and the corporate community are available for implementation. It is time to unveil our eyes, see things from His perspective and prepare the way of the Lord.

EIGHT

≈

STEWARDS OF THE
LAND AND CITY

The Canadian newspaper *The Globe and Mail* printed a fascinating article on November 28, 1998, entitled "Natural Disaster Costs Soar to World Record." The subhead of this article stated, "Study blames deforestation and human meddling for 1998's $130 billion in damages." The newspaper reported that violent weather had resulted in major disasters throughout the decade of the 1980s, but that more money was spent for disaster relief in 1998 alone than in all the other years put together. Human meddling in nature was to blame for much of this $130 billion loss, which came from storms, floods, droughts and fires, and resulted in an estimated 32,000 people being killed and another 300 million being displaced—more than the entire population of the United States.

A spokesman for Worldwatch, an environmental research group, was quoted as saying, "More and more, there's a human fingerprint in natural disasters in that we're making them more frequent and more intense and we're also ...making them more destructive." This spokesman, Seth Dunn, a research associate and climate change expert at the institute, went on to explain:

When hillsides are left bare, rainfall will rush across the land
or into rivers without being slowed by trees and allowed to be
absorbed by the soil or [to] evaporate back into the atmosphere. This leads to floods and landslides that are strong enough
to wipe out roads, farms and fisheries far downstream. In a
sense, we're turning up the faucets . . . and throwing away the
sponges like the forests and the wetlands.

Thus even secular newspapers are giving testimony to our
neglect as stewards! We have not been vigilant to take hold of
our mandate; and the land and people are suffering for it. That
is the bad news. The good news is, the effects of our sin committed on the land—war, famine, disease, ecological devastation—are used by God to catch our attention so that our fallen
stewardship can be addressed, the land can be healed and God's
purposes for His land and people can be released.

What will we do with the mandate given us as servants of
the Kingdom of God? We are challenged with this question
in the parables—the expression of Jesus' theology about the
Kingdom of God.

What the Parables Teach Us

Matthew 25:14–30 relays Jesus' parable of the talents. It is
a familiar passage concerning three servants, all of whom were
given various talents—each worth more than a thousand dollars—according to their respective abilities. The master praised
the first two for sound investment but condemned the third
for digging a hole in the ground and hiding his talent. Jesus
concluded:

"His master replied, 'You wicked, lazy servant! So you knew
that I harvest where I have not sown and gather where I have
not scattered seed? Well then, you should have put my money

on deposit with the bankers, so that when I returned I would have received it back with interest.

"'Take the talent from him and give it to the one who has the ten talents. For everyone who has will be given more, and he will have an abundance. Whoever does not have, even what he has will be taken from him. And throw that worthless servant outside, into the darkness, where there will be weeping and gnashing of teeth.'"

Matthew 25:26–30

This parable makes the point that Jesus expects results from our stewardship, and God expects His people to use wisdom and perseverance as we wait for the full consummation of His Kingdom in our midst.

While we watch and wait, conflict is taking place in the heavenlies. What we see and experience in the physical realm is a reflection of what is taking place in the spiritual realm. Again, it is a matter of worldview. A biblical worldview reveals responsibility and decision-making. Parables like the Good Samaritan (see Luke 10:25–37) and the rich man and Lazarus (see Luke 16:19–31) expose the radical difference between the Kingdom of God and our daily experience. The choice is ours—whether, individually and corporately, we choose to live as stewards of the Kingdom of God.

Linthicum, in his biblical theology of the urban church, concurs that the call has been made to Christians to go to work:

> Christians can work pragmatically on behalf of the kingdom of God right where they are, proclaiming the Good News with their lips, by their actions, and in their lives as they seek to be responsive to the particular needs and problems of the people in their neighborhoods, cities, and nations.[1]

No wonder that in the stewardship parables, God asks us to reclaim what has been lost, hidden or stolen. This is the mandate entrusted to us as servants of the Kingdom. God has made

211

available to us, as His servants and friends, all that we require to redeem our defilement of His stewardship. We can have the privilege of redeeming it in a manner that reflects His glory and purpose in the lives of His people, and as reflected on His land.

Checklists for Healthy Stewardship

I live near one of the most beautiful cities in the world—Victoria, British Columbia, Canada. Several years ago Dr. C. Peter Wagner and I stood on the top of a hill overlooking Victoria. It is a stunning setting, adjacent to the ocean, protected by the Cascade and Olympic Mountain ranges. As we reflected on the scene, I could not help commenting to Dr. Wagner, "Yes, it looks beautiful, but Victoria is rather like *Beauty and the Beast*. Everything looks all right, but there's a darker side that is quite sinister."

Indeed, any city can look fresh and clean on the outside, but harbor an evil or ominous power at work on the inside poisoning the lives of the inhabitants. Once again from Linthicum's *City of God, City of Satan*:

> Every city has a "spirit" about it—an almost palpable essence distinct from every other city. It is a combination of that city's history, surroundings, and systems, even people who have moved through it, and events that have occurred in it. If we cannot name, understand, and cope with our city's spirit, we cannot hope to understand either the complexity of our city's spiritual warfare, or the scope of ministry to which the church is called.[2]

Here is the crucial point: In order for a church to carry on effective ministry (stewardship) in a city, it needs to understand the systems of that city. Time and time again God has spoken to His people through the prophets, highlighting the extent of their sin and the effect it has had on their land:

The land is full of adulterers; because of the curse the land lies parched and the pastures in the desert are withered. The prophets follow an evil course and use their power unjustly.

Jeremiah 23:10

If we are to distinguish between Beauty and the Beast, are there simplified or practical ways to evaluate the spiritual fabric of a city?

Our ministry teams have determined ways to navigate the spiritual contours of any community. The following four sets of checklists combine study and practical ministry that have been collated over the years, based on many church and city projects. They give at least initial insight into the reality of life as seen through the eyes of the Lord in that area.

The Health of Your Church

This checklist indicates the extent to which the enemy of God's people has gained access to the life of the local church. Bear in mind that the church is the sign of God's Kingdom in a local community. This checklist helps us monitor the state of the local church in the conflict between the Kingdom of God and the kingdom of the world.

- Is there a history of church splits within the fellowship?
- Is there a history of leadership problems or relationship issues within the board/council/elders?
- Is there a lack of focused vision? (Does the church as a whole own the vision?)
- Is there a history of music or worship problems?
- Is there a history of constant financial worries or frustrations?
- Has there been an inability to retain Sunday school/youth ministry growth over the years? Growth comes, but then it is lost?

213

- Have there ever been leadership marriage splits?
- Is there a history of leadership indiscretion?
- Has it been hard to maintain spiritual growth?
- Has there been little success at community outreach and evangelism over the years?
- What is the historical involvement of other churches in interchurch events?
- Has there been backbiting, gossip or general discontent? Does this occasionally recur?
- Has there been a history of sickness or illness, especially within leadership families?
- Has there been effective conversion growth (not transfer or biological growth) over the years?

We have found these to be the most common issues requiring attention until stewardship needs are addressed. Leaders tend to develop depression, despair and discouragement; often they leave. It is hard to advance the Kingdom until such issues are resolved.

The Health of Your Business

This checklist determines the most likely issues that will arise, especially within a Christian-based business, if defilement and sin lie at the foundation and have never been addressed.

- Is there substantial employee turnover?
- What is the general feeling about job satisfaction?
- Do the employees reflect high self-esteem?
- Has there been a history of grumbling, backbiting or even jealousy?
- Have there ever been occurrences of internal theft?
- How is productivity? the profit margin?

214

- Do people ever jockey for position?
- Has there ever been any evidence of occult activity?
- What about absenteeism? Is this normal or higher than average?
- Have there ever been any cases of sexual abuse?
- Have there ever been any unusual trade union problems?
- Have there ever been occurrences of confusion among the leadership or management?
- Has the business ever been subject to a hostile takeover?

Any or all of these issues can mean that the spiritual fabric of one's business or company needs to be examined prayerfully and carefully.

The Health of the Education Sector

These questions indicate some of the areas of concern within schools and colleges that often reflect issues within the community. People in education, both students and teachers, are among the most influenced and influential in any given area.

- Has there ever been any occult or New Age activity in the schools?
- Has there ever been a history of intimidation and bullying by either students or staff?
- Has there been any history of, or potential for, gangs?
- Has the influence of educational or library materials ever been questionable?
- Has there been a history of negative student-teacher co-operation?
- Has there ever been a lack of parent-teacher cooperation?
- Has there ever been, or does there tend to be, excessive absenteeism?

215

- Has there been frequent damage or a lack of respect for school property?
- Has there been a history or appearance of sexual promiscuity by either staff or students?
- Are drugs or alcohol used in education facilities?
- What is the history of the family unit breakup within the local school situation?
- Has there ever been evidence of cultural friction between people groups within the schools or colleges?

The Health of the Political Sector

This area can be most influential in any community. Politicians can either influence structures and systems or be influenced by them. The following checklist enables us to determine whether the influences in a community are positive or negative.

- Has there been a history of political instability or continual changeovers?
- Has there ever been significant indiscretion by participants in the political process?
- Has there ever been any in-house favoritism over certain issues?
- Has there been a lack of accountability on the part of public servants?
- Are people within the political arena easily led by "strongmen"—people who wield unique influence in the area?
- Have there ever been cases of personal avarice at the expense of the entire community?
- Are any members of the political arena influenced by non-Christian spirituality?
- Has there ever been any specific abrasiveness against the Christian Church?

• Has there ever been any harassment against Christian politicians?

Ways to Maintain Vigilance

Being good and faithful stewards of any community requires vigilance in order that the footholds of the enemy are addressed quickly and removed. Careful research and prayer within these four areas—church, business, education and politics—enable us to determine where spiritual darkness has settled, how it grew, and how it can be addressed and removed.

Again, it is important to remove the birds, thorns and rocks so that the seed of the Kingdom can sprout and grow.

Guard, Keep and Occupy!

We have learned a succession of steps to spiritual cleansing. Now we must learn to *guard, keep* and *occupy* in order to retain Beauty and remove the Beast.

And, if I may change the metaphor, it means that we often find ourselves, as stewards, involved in fruit inspection. Jesus said:

> "By their fruit you will recognize them. Do people pick grapes from thornbushes, or figs from thistles? Likewise every good tree bears good fruit, but a bad tree bears bad fruit. A good tree cannot bear bad fruit, and a bad tree cannot bear good fruit. Every tree that does not bear good fruit is cut down and thrown into the fire. *Thus, by their fruit you will recognize them.*"

> Matthew 7:16–20, emphasis added

Stewards must be willing to implement Matthew 3:10:"The ax is already at the root of the trees, and every tree that does

217

not produce good fruit will be cut down and thrown into the fire." In observing the ministry of the March for Jesus, for which I serve as chaplain to the national board of Canada, I have found that it is not always easy to sustain the quality and size of the marches, which are held worldwide, from one year to the next. Often we hear the same report from different localities around the globe: A successful march is followed by difficulties and problems, resulting in a weaker march the following year.

It is usually in the area of relationships that pressures arise following a successful march. Issues of apathy, individualism, aloofness, competitiveness and even jealousy can arise between members of a leadership board who were working together the previous year with significant unity and common vision. The recognition of this bad fruit shows that even wonderful, godly ministries are susceptible to a slackening of watchfulness.

We must not let down our guard. Here is where we need to understand the spiritual principle found in Matthew 12:43–45 (also Luke 11:24–26):

> "When an evil spirit comes out of a man, it goes through arid places seeking rest and does not find it. Then it says, 'I will return to the house I left.' When it arrives, it finds the house unoccupied, swept clean and put in order. Then it goes and takes with it seven other spirits more wicked than itself, and they go in and live there. And the final condition of that man is worse than the first."

This teaching is often connected with individual discipleship, but it is equally applicable to corporate ministry, and a vital complement to our work of spiritual cleansing. It is one thing to cleanse our lives and the land; it is quite another to maintain and occupy what we have gained so that the enemy cannot return. But if we intend to cleanse, we must occupy.

Philippians 4:7 promises that "the peace of God ... will guard your hearts and your minds in Christ Jesus." This word *guard* has a military pedigree. It really means "to garrison." So we are to set up a guard or garrison over whatever God has entrusted to us, whatever we are responsible for on His behalf. Then we will be fruitful in reaching cities for His Kingdom:

> "Enlarge the place of your tent, stretch your tent curtains wide, do not hold back; lengthen your cords, strengthen your stakes. For you will spread out to the right and to the left; your descendants will dispossess nations and settle in their desolate cities."
>
> Isaiah 54:2–3

Attain, Maintain and Retain!

Now we move to the next step, also related to vigilance: Whatever we *attain* for Christ, we must *maintain* in order to *retain*.

This is done through prayer and relationships involving intercessors and church leaders. It may involve an increased number of Concerts of Prayer, or whatever form of public unity is right for deploying the custodianship of the Church over the city. It requires being attentive to misunderstandings in relationships in order that the enemy not achieve any foothold.

Enlarging the place of our tent in the local setting requires an increase in our stewardship responsibility. If we are to invest wisely what He has entrusted to us, we need to heed an idea we reflected on earlier: "From everyone who has been given much, much will be demanded; and from the one who has been entrusted with much, much more will be asked" (Luke 12:48).

When a person comes to Christ, or when a March for Jesus takes place, or when a church conducts a joint mission with fellow congregations, or when we have any sense of spiritual breakthrough in the community, this is when we are at our most vulnerable and when we must retain what we have won.

219

Our areas of greatest strength, as we saw in chapter 5, can also be our areas of greatest vulnerability. Faithful stewardship means being willing to guard, keep and occupy in order to maintain what we have attained, in order to retain it. In this way a *visitation* of God can lead to His *habitation* in our midst (recall 2 Chronicles 7:15–16).

This constitutes *spiritual retention* or *preservation*—an essential tool in maintaining ongoing community transformation.

Spiritual "Twinning"

Now a warning.

Our connectedness with others is key to our fruitfulness in stewardship. Paul makes clear that we must be holy and unde-filed in all our relationships, since there can be no union "between the temple of God and idols" (2 Corinthians 6:16). "Do not be yoked together with unbelievers," he warns. "For what do righteousness and wickedness have in common? Or what fellowship can light have with darkness?" (verse 14).

If God is to live and work among His people, we can tolerate no unclean thing in our midst. We have seen this theme again and again in various Old Testament passages. Ponder again the words of Leviticus 18:26–27:

> "You must keep my decrees and my laws. The native-born and the aliens living among you must not do any of these detestable things, for all these things were done by the people who lived in the land before you, and the land became defiled."

Ezra 9:1–2 gives the further clarification of the necessity of not being yoked with other people or nations:

> ... The leaders came to me and said, "The people of Israel, including the priests and the Levites, have not kept themselves

separate from the neighboring peoples with their detestable practices ... They have ... mingled the holy race with the peoples around them. And the leaders and officials have led the way in this unfaithfulness."

As with some of the earlier Scriptures, these verses are often applied to individuals. But since cities and nations comprise people, a corporate truth also applies to our study and to a practice currently taking place.

Officials and politicians of a given community will sometimes undertake a process called "twinning" with an overseas community. Another name for this is developing a "sister" relationship. The rationale behind it is one of friendship, understanding and relationship-building. It can be a positive and strengthening experience for both "twins." In many cases, however, the people involved are unaware of the spiritual ramifications of such activity. This reality should not be overlooked by those who are aware of the place of stewardship in their communities.

We have already determined that there is a spiritual influence behind all that goes on in the physical realm around us. Doesn't it make sense that if we physically twin with another city, we can also take on the spiritual characteristics, and become susceptible to the newly imported spiritual influence, of that place? This can have a positive effect on both communities and cities, but it can have negative ramifications, too.

Some years ago our ministry team was asked to conduct a seminar in a city in North America that was well known for its tourism. Issues of apathy and disunity had begun to develop within the churches of that city. Then we learned that the city officials had recently twinned their city in partnership with a community in Japan. As a gift, the Japanese community sent Shinto gates, which were now situated at the entrance to the North American city. And because of this "spiritual yoking," the gates had become a vehicle of communication with, and influence from, the spirits of Shintoism in the Japanese city. In due course the tourism industry began to decline, as did some of the commercial activities in the area, along with a distinct deterioration in church unity.

To many in the Church, such a connection strains credulity; but to us the cause and effect were obvious. In recent conversation with one of the mobilizing pastors of that city, I learned that there is now a deeper understanding of the spiritual issues of twinning and of the impact that this has had within the churches and within the city itself over the past few years. A new rallying together of pastors and intercessors is taking place, with an awareness of what must be addressed and a determination to reach the city for Christ.

As a further example, the city of Middlesbrough in England is twinned with three other communities—Dunkerque in France, Masvingo in Zimbabwe and Oberhausen in Germany. Are the people who live in these four communities aware of the spiritual pedigree that has now been given access to all four of them?

The file in my office on twinned cities grows regularly with questions and concerns over such spiritual yoking. It is important that the gatekeepers and watchmen of cities keep vigilance over the various forms of influence we allow over our lives, our cities and our land. How well do *you*, as a steward of the land, know *your* city? This is what faithful stewardship is all about.

Watchmen and Gatekeepers

In most present-day prayer circles, intercessors are regarded as the watchmen of a city. In many cases, though, watchmen are not only intercessors but leaders. The watchman is the person who stands before God on behalf of the land so He does not have to destroy it because of its sin (see Ezekiel 22:30). The watchmen are also those posted to stand in the gap between God and His people, to intervene on their behalf and to sound the alarm when the enemy launches an attack. As Ezekiel 3:17 states, "Son of man, I have made you a watchman for the house of Israel; so hear the word I speak and give them warning from me."

With the increase of intercessors in the Church today, it seems prudent for each church to release a number of intercessors to be responsible for praying for their cities regularly. Then, if the alarm is sounded for any reason, they can alert the leadership right away, and the people can seek God's counsel on what has to be done.

In an emerging number of cities, people have prayed strategically for Christians to be voted into the position of mayor. I know of some cities in North America in which the mayors (mostly Christian) consult regularly with the pastors of the city in an ongoing exchange of prayer and preparation, seeking God's counsel together. When issues arise that concern either the mayor or the pastors, they can address the situation quickly and prayerfully together.

Gatekeepers of the city do not consist only of clergy and pastors. They include politicians, educators, economists, health officials, media personnel and certain indigenous laypersons. Gatekeepers are people of influence who can readily determine the ebb and flow of what goes on in the life of their city. From Scripture we learn that they are to protect the city, to make decisions concerning it, to discern what is right and wrong, to determine the city's direction, to govern it (at times spiritually), to allow or deny entry to whatever form of influence seeks to enter it, to remain vigilant at all times and not to leave their posts.

Nehemiah acknowledged the importance of gatekeepers following the rebuilding of the wall: "The gates of Jerusalem are not to be opened until the sun is hot. While the gatekeepers are still on duty, have them shut the doors and bar them" (Nehemiah 7:3). First Chronicles 26 also gives insight into the responsibilities of gatekeepers. *Gatekeepers execute extraordinary authority in the city* and can appropriate Matthew

18:18–20 on a corporate basis—for binding and loosing, and for asking the Father, in agreement, for anything in Jesus' name.

Emeka Nwankpa, in his book *Redeeming the Land*, offers some insights about gates that help us understand the importance of gatekeepers:

> In real life, gates provide protection. So we must understand that every city in the spiritual realm has gates. The enemy, in order to keep certain lands, cities, towns, villages, provinces under his control, has gates. And these gates are there to protect what is inside. The Book of Joshua (2:5–7) describes Jericho's high gates. It was one of the cities that the Children of Israel had to conquer. In the Bible, whenever the gates of a city are destroyed, it means that particular city has fallen into disgrace. In the Book of Nehemiah (1:3; 3:3) we read of the reports he received. One of the things that saddened Nehemiah was the destruction of the gates of Jerusalem. In spiritual warfare, in redeeming land, we must pay attention to the gates. Gates exist in the natural (physical) and in the spiritual realm.[3]

Nwankpa points out that the New Testament addresses gates, too. In the book of Acts (for example, Acts 12:10 and 16:26) we read that God had various ways of dealing with the issue of gates, including sending an angel to open them. Nwankpa adds that "gates may apply to a city, town, province, business, factory, and even a church."[4]

Think of the extraordinary spiritual authority available at every level of city life if watchmen and gatekeepers follow through on the execution of their responsibilities as faithful stewards of God's people!

Walking and Working in Unity

In Matthew 4:21 we read of Jesus calling His first disciples. Two of them, James and John, were preparing their nets. The

Greek word used here is *katartismos*, meaning "to realign or to mend," so that there are no holes that can weaken the strength of the net. The same Greek word is found in Ephesians 4:12 in connection with the ministries responsible "to prepare God's people for works of service, so that the body of Christ may be built up until we all reach unity in the faith" (Ephesians 4:12–13). In this instance *katartismos* means "to prepare, to perfect, to coach and to encourage."

Preparation and encouragement are taking place at all levels of the Church today as Christ builds and unifies His Body in a way that reflects His glory and honor.

Ephesians 4 mentions two kinds of unity: "the unity of the Spirit" (verse 3) and "unity in the faith" (verse 13). It is virtually impossible for the corporate Church to enjoy unity in the faith until we first walk in the unity of the Spirit. This is what praying with unity is all about. It does not mean unanimous prayer; it means majoring on the strengths of what is common in our calling as the Body of Christ, praying in the one Spirit Jesus referred to in His prayer in John 17:20–23.

When Jesus offered up that extraordinary prayer, He was asking the Father that we might experience the same relationship that He and the Father experience.

The degree to which we are in relationship with each other is the degree to which the world will know that Jesus is who He says He is. This is an astounding expectation on Jesus' part! Yet it emphasizes the depth of His love for us and the responsibility we have as stewards of His grace.

Looking at John 17, we can see many characteristics that Jesus modeled during His years of ministry on earth. These include holiness, accountability to the Father, humility, integrity and transparency. Paul taught Titus that when we show integrity, nobody will have anything bad to say about us (see Titus 2:7–8). And our transparency with each other minimizes whatever foothold the devil may try to get in our lives (see Ephesians 4:25–28). Transparency means honesty and openness and a willingness to be in full relationship with others.

225

John 17, coupled with Psalm 133, that wonderful overture to unity with one another, becomes the perfect antidote to the assault being waged on our lives. This is what walking and working in unity is all about. It is how we will see our cities and land with unveiled eyes, and gain entry in the name of the Lord. It is when we reach this point in our corporate relationships as the Body of Christ that we will experience the promise of the psalmist: "*There* the Lord bestows [or commands] his blessing, even life forevermore" (Psalm 133:3, emphasis added). This is what is involved in being faithful stewards of God's land and the city. This is why we must see His land with unveiled eyes.

The words of Exodus 19:5 should resonate with all of us and reside at the deepest level of our being: "Although the whole earth is mine, you will be for me a kingdom of priests and a holy nation."

NINE

WITH UNVEILED EYES

We, who with unveiled faces all reflect the Lord's glory, are being transformed into his likeness with ever-increasing glory, which comes from the Lord, who is the Spirit.

2 Corinthians 3:18

Reflecting God's glory is surely the desire of every Christian. But before we can have unveiled eyes, we must first have unveiled faces. No sin or defilement must mar or prevent the glory of Christ from shining on and within the whole of our lives. As the veil of sin and unbelief is removed from our faces and from our relationship with God, we can behold and reflect His glory in who we are and in what we do.

In this book we have taken an in-depth look at the healing of land, and have addressed the problem of 2 Corinthians 4:4: "The god of this age has blinded the minds of unbelievers, so that they cannot see the light of the gospel of the glory of Christ, who is the image of God." Faithful stewardship will result in unveiled eyes, unveiled faces, unveiled hearts.

Paul puts it this way in Ephesians 1:18: "I pray also that the eyes of your heart may be enlightened in order that you may know the hope to which [God] has called you, the riches of his glorious inheritance in the saints." It is obvious that Paul wants us to see things from God's perspective and to be transformed in our relationship with Him—spirit, soul and body.

As we saw in the last chapter, what is true of the individual is also true of the community. We are living in the day of the Christian Church when transformed communities are becoming a reality.

Transformed Communities

> Give the king [knowledge of] Your way of judging, O God, and [the spirit of] Your righteousness to the king's son [to control all his actions].
>
> Psalm 72:1, AMP

My training as an Anglican pastor taught me about pastoring a church, not an entire community. In a local church one can identify positive changes fairly readily. But what about the concept of an entire city being reached for Christ? Can we expect to see widespread change once certain factors in any sized community are addressed? What exactly does a transformed community look like?

In January 2000 I was visiting an area in South London that has been the subject of much strategic and collective prayer on the part of the local church body. I was aware of an atmosphere much more peaceful than in other areas of Greater London I had visited. That may seem subjective, but I found it interesting to learn of the reduction in crime and poverty that has taken place in concert with the prayer strategy over the last few years. What has developed is a wider acceptance to the Church as a whole, with less resistance to the Church's involvement in much of the community's life. A combination of intercessory prayer and prayer walks had been implemented on an ongoing basis, and I sensed welcome and warmth in the area.

Is this what a transformed community looks like? We can certainly call it a community in the *process* of transformation. What evidence of fruit do we look for that gives us the impression that God's presence is being attracted to a specific area?

Change at Every Level

In chapter 7 I mentioned that some fascinating developments have taken place in Hemet, California. Pastor Bob Beckett cites ways his home city has entered a significant time of change. He tells, for instance, the story of a canyon in their valley known as Massacre Canyon.

About 350 years ago hundreds of women, children and elderly men of the Soboba Indian tribe were slaughtered in this canyon by the Pachanga tribe. In 1990, following spiritual mapping research and extensive prayer, a solemn assembly was called, including Christian representatives of both tribes. Identificational repentance and the remitting of sins took place, and holy Communion was celebrated. "Since that summer day in 1990," Beckett writes in *Commitment to Conquer*, "there has not been a single inter-tribal murder, in spite of the past reputation of violence on the reservation—a reputation that no longer exists."[1]

Beckett also recounts that some years ago, corporate irresponsibility and agricultural destruction left the Soboba Indian reservation without water. The shamans responded by cursing the company that was exporting water out of the valley in the 1930s. They also cursed some of the company workers, who then began to die under strange circumstances. When Beckett first arrived in Hemet, it was a dry, arid place. Again a solemn assembly was held, and sins were remitted between the Sobobas and the water company. Many Sobobas have now become Christians, and the valley has since enjoyed record rain levels.[2]

The testimony of Hemet, California, also includes extensive church growth and wonderful pastoral unity, to the degree
that the ministers see themselves as pastoring not just their individual churches but the city as a whole. Crime and drugs
have begun to decrease, and several gang members have become Christians.[3]

Is this what a transformed community looks like? Again, as
in the case of the community in Greater London, the city of
Hemet is in the *process* of transformation, and its fruit provides
evidence of a root change that is having a significant effect at
all levels of community life.

It is debatable whether a city or a nation could ever be fully
transformed this side of heaven. We know that the New
Jerusalem is a promise awaiting every Christian. Yet is it not
possible that a reflection of what is yet to come can be experienced now, as the Kingdom of God impacts the kingdoms of
this world? As people change, their cities and nations change,
too. The degree to which they change is the degree to which
we see transformation taking place at all levels of society.

The Fruit of Transformation

Many years ago I was pastoring a church that was unaware
of such terms as spiritual mapping and identificational repentance. Our experience was one of minimal church growth, and
we had little impact on the community as a whole. Only after
certain research was undertaken, more directive prayer was
launched, and specific sins on the land were addressed, repented
of, forgiven and cleansed, did we begin to experience many
conversions and significant church growth. The finances and
the caliber of worship in our church began to improve dra-
matically. God was teaching us the significance of 2 Corinthians 3:18 and 2 Corinthians 4:4. Indeed, we began to see veils
being removed from eyes and hearts so that we could all behold "the gospel of the glory of Christ," both personally and

corporately. And the community as a whole acknowledged the church's existence and contribution to the people of the community.

Community transformation means that a community or city is experiencing transformation socially, politically, economically, spiritually—at *every* level, not simply in areas of church growth.

In *The Twilight Labyrinth* George Otis describes how transformation has become a reality in several communities formerly ravaged by sin and unbelief, such as in Kiambu, Kenya (also referred to in chapter 7). Kiambu was under the stronghold of a witch named Mama Jane who ran a divination house, Emmanuel Clinic. Her witchcraft was the power behind many problems in Kiambu, including lack of church growth and untimely deaths due to accidents, murder and crime. A pastor in Kiambu, Thomas Muthee, talked with Otis:

> "Mama Jane has been gone about four years," Thomas told me in 1996. "We have not had a single accident during this time. In fact, since this woman moved out of Kiambu, the entire atmosphere has changed. Whereas people used to be afraid to go out at night, now we enjoy one of the lowest crime rates in the country. Rape and murder are virtually unheard of anymore. The economy has also started to grow. . . . Now that Kiambu has a good name, people from Nairobi are flocking to get houses here."[4]

The breakthrough in Kiambu came when Thomas and his wife prayed strategically against the power of witchcraft that had to be removed before transformation could begin.

A video produced by The Sentinel Group, *Transformations*, has had an extraordinary effect on the Church in many parts of the world.[5] Apart from showing these amazing reports from Hemet and Kiambu, as well as from Cali, Colombia, and Almolonga, Guatemala, it has afforded people a visual glance at what does happen when the Church prays knowledgeably concerning the issues that lie at the heart of her communities. In every case referred to in this video, a variety of strongholds and bondages were addressed by the Church. All were based on different levels of sin that had become entrenched in the spiritual terrain, causing a variety of serious problems in each community.

Similar testimonies are coming forth from neighborhoods, towns, cities and regions all over the world, in such areas as India, Siberia, Alaska, the Arctic in northern Canada, as well as in South Africa and the South Pacific, to name but a few. Cities of all sizes are experiencing united prayer services with large numbers of people attending. Enthusiasm for transformation is growing at an exponential rate worldwide. The Church universal is engaged in one of the most profound movements of prayer ever recorded in history. She is laying claim to this familiar promise in Scripture with renewed vigor and expectancy:

> "I tell you the truth, whatever you bind on earth will be bound in heaven, and whatever you loose on earth will be loosed in heaven. Again, I tell you that if two of you on earth agree about anything you ask for, it will be done for you by my Father in heaven."
>
> Matthew 18:18–19

As goes the Church, so goes the world.

These are just a few of the testimonies emerging from different parts of the world in which communities have begun to experience transformation. In a number of them, several of the transformation principles referred to in Leviticus 26 have become reality. God is showing His Church the importance of understanding land from His perspective and learning how to cleanse it. Land can be healed, and the eyes and hearts of the people who live on it freed to behold the glory of God. Let's declare this good news to every city and nation—indeed, to the land!

Prophesy to the Land

Ezekiel 22:3–5 explains that the house of Israel was in serious trouble:

> "This is what the Sovereign LORD says: O city that brings
> on herself doom by shedding blood in her midst and defiles
> herself by making idols, you have become guilty because of the
> blood you have shed and have become defiled by the idols you
> have made. You have brought your days to a close, and the end
> of your years has come. Therefore I will make you an object
> of scorn to the nations and a laughingstock to all the coun-
> tries. Those who are near and those who are far away will mock
> you, O infamous city, full of turmoil."

Once again the people had defiled the land by engaging in
each of the four major sins: idolatry, immorality, bloodshed and
the breaking of covenants. In addition the princes, priests,
prophets, officials—indeed, all the people of the land—were
involved in these injustices (see verses 25–29).

The word of the Lord came to Ezekiel several times, but
look at the directive in verse 24: "Son of man, *say to the land,*
'You are a land that has had no rain or showers in the day of
wrath'" (emphasis added). The prophet was called to speak
forth to the land. This is a cry that has echoed in the hearts of
men and women of God through the ages.

One of the famous "preaching verses" of George White-
field, the eighteenth-century evangelist and John Wesley associate who stimulated revival throughout many churches in
Britain and America, was Jeremiah 22:29: "O land, land, land,
hear the word of the LORD!"

God often calls His servants to speak forth, or prophesy, to
the land. We find an extraordinary example in Ezekiel 36. God
called His prophet several times to speak to the land, giving the
land numerous promises, including fruitfulness, harvest, the
multiplication of people, the rebuilding of towns and coming

prosperity for both people and land. But He also offered a timely reminder concerning the sin and fallen stewardship of the people: "Son of man, when the people of Israel were living in their own land, they defiled it by their conduct and their actions. Their conduct was like a woman's monthly uncleanness in my sight" (verse 17).

In the following four verses Ezekiel continued to declare the word of God, describing the consequences of the people's sinful behavior. Their fallen stewardship had caused them to be scattered in many places, and they were judged according to their conduct. God's holy name had been "profaned" (verse 21).

Then promises of transformation were extended—extraordinary assurances of cleansing, renewal, deliverance and healing:

> "I will take you out of the nations; I will gather you from all the countries and bring you back into your own land. I will sprinkle clean water on you, and you will be clean; I will cleanse you from all your impurities and from all your idols. I will give you a new heart and put a new spirit in you; I will remove from you your heart of stone and give you a heart of flesh.... You will live in the land I gave your forefathers; you will be my people, and I will be your God. I will save you from all your uncleanness. I will call for the grain and make it plentiful and will not bring famine upon you. I will increase the fruit of the trees and the crops of the field, so that you will no longer suffer disgrace among the nations because of famine."
>
> verses 24–26, 28–30

Verse 35 declares the transformation of both land and people: "This land that was laid waste has become like the garden of Eden; the cities that were lying in ruins, desolate and destroyed, are now fortified and inhabited." The nations were being informed that it was God doing the rebuilding and replanting (see verse 36). And the result: The land, the people and the cities would all be cleansed, renewed, reformed and rebuilt. In other words, people's *deficiency* was dealt with through God's *sufficiency,* and then their redeemed *efficiency* became their *proficiency* for God's work.

The prophet declared the result:

> "This is what the Sovereign LORD says: Once again I will yield to the plea of the house of Israel and do this for them: I will make their people as numerous as sheep, as numerous as the flocks for offerings at Jerusalem during her appointed feasts. So will the ruined cities be filled with flocks of people. Then they will know that I am the LORD."

> verses 37–38

The Revised Standard Version puts verse 37 this way: "This also I will let the house of Israel ask me to do for them: *to increase their men like a flock*" (emphasis added). Today we call this evangelism! Putting it another way: The process of cleansing and renewal moves God to respond to the prayers of His people.

Community transformation, therefore, is not only possible, but a characteristic of God's delight. As relationships between people and God and between people and people are dealt with, and as their fallen stewardship that has taken place on the land is removed and cleansed, then the eyes of the people in that land can be opened to the Gospel. The healing of land results in people's responding to the Gospel and the presence of God dwelling in their midst. The promise is a new heart, a new spirit, a new people.

Why does God care about the land? Recall that God created it for His good pleasure. Colossians 1:16: "By him all things were created: things in heaven and on earth, visible and invisible, whether thrones or powers or rulers or authorities; all things were created by him and for him." Revelation 4:11 gives this testimony: "You are worthy, our Lord and God, to receive glory and honor and power, for you created all things, and by your will they were created and have their being." No wonder God is "jealous for His land" (Joel 2:18) and "saw that it was good" (Genesis 1:10).

He weeps over the land as He witnesses its devastation as a result of our defilement (Jeremiah 9:10). Yet it has always been His purpose, since His original mandate to Adam, to involve us in its stewardship. Psalm 115:16 says, "The highest heavens belong to the LORD, but the earth he has given to man." Through the work of Jesus Christ, God has given us the responsibility of cleansing and redeeming the land, then returning it to Him for His Kingdom purposes. He promises that "houses, fields and vineyards will again be bought in this land" (Jeremiah 32:15).

As we speak forth God's Word, acknowledging our work and responsibility as His stewards, the land will respond to His Word (see Psalm 18:7; 97:1–6). It will again yield its harvest for God, according to the promises of Ezekiel 36, once we have undertaken our stewardship responsibility. The words of Zechariah 3:9–10 express the heart of God:

> "... I will remove the sin of this land in a single day. In that day each of you will invite his neighbor to sit under his vine and fig tree," declares the LORD Almighty.

A Road Much Traveled

Stewardship of the land is both an exciting and a solemn responsibility. We have determined in our study of stewardship that land reflects the character and nature of God. Sin defiles the land, and there are ramifications of such sin that need to be addressed by each of us as God's stewards. In this way land is cleansed, redeemed and healed. This, in turn, leads to the transformation of communities, which yields the blessings of God for His people.

We have also learned that although the "god of this age has blinded the minds of unbelievers," it is possible to address this issue even on a corporate basis, and undertake ministry that will change the spiritual nature of a community, resulting in a potential increase of effective evangelism. The steward of God has a responsibility placed before him that cannot be overlooked!

In the words of Loren Wilkinson:

> To call humans "stewards of God" is to claim implicitly that humans are accountable—that is, *responsible* to God. In giving men and women dominion over the earth, God has made them answerable for the way in which they use that dominion. And, as far as we know, such accountability is unique to humanity.[6]

Paul also refers in Ephesians 3:2 to "the stewardship of God's grace that was given to me for you, how the mystery was made known to me by revelation" (RSV). Writes Douglas John Hall:

> The new dimension in this important passage is what we may call the dimension of participation. Although a steward of God (or Christ), like the stewards of earthly lords, can claim nothing for him or herself, that steward is not merely an outsider—hired help, so to speak. Rather the steward participates in the very "household of God." As such, the steward is "called" and "enabled" to share His grace (v. 8) with others, and to bring them in turn into God's household.[7]

Stewards are undoubtedly people of influence, whether for good or for bad. God has called us to reclaim for Him what is rightfully His, and to increase and maintain our stewardship on an ongoing basis.

It is our inheritance and mandate, as stewards acting on behalf of the owner of the resources of the land, to clear the land of rocks and thorns and to keep the spiritual birds at bay, in order to maximize the harvest. It is also our mandate to ensure that we who are on a road much traveled "remove the obstacles out of the way of my people" (Isaiah 57:14), some of these put there by those who have gone before us, and prepare the road for those who are yet to follow—a people prepared for the Lord.

Indeed, it is an extraordinary authority that we have been given from God. The psalmist describes our mandate this way:

> You made [man] a little lower than the heavenly beings and crowned him with glory and honor. You made him ruler over the works of your hands; you put everything under his feet: all flocks and herds, and the beasts of the field, the birds of the air, and the fish of the sea, all that swim the paths of the seas.
>
> Psalm 8:5–8

We have been given dominion over nature, and are to use this dominion to serve humanity, nature and God Himself. As we seek to exercise it, let's look at some practical ways we can pray and work toward opening the eyes and ears of our communities to the Lord, enabling them to respond to the one who stands knocking at the door.

The Doors to a City

> Not many sounds in life, and I include all urban and all rural sounds, exceed in interest a knock at the door.
>
> Charles Lamb

Hezekiah became king of Judah at the young age of 25, taking over from his evil father, Ahaz. Ahaz had brought much sin into Jerusalem and on the land. But Hezekiah "did what was right in the eyes of the LORD" (2 Chronicles 29:2).

At the start of his reign he opened the doors of the Temple and repaired them. He assembled the priests and Levites and told them to consecrate themselves, to consecrate the Temple and to "remove all defilement from the sanctuary" (verse 5). This fascinating chapter, describing the purification of the Temple, gives us a glimpse of Hezekiah's urgency to ensure that God's house be freed from defilement so it could be available once again for the work of the Lord.

Like Hezekiah we must open and repair the doors—in this case, not the doors to the Temple but the doors to the city. There are at least six major doorways into which we must enter and pray if we want to reach a community.

The Church Door

The first is the door of the local church. The church uses this door to minister to other local churches in the area.

Numbers of cities are now experiencing the power of a united, praying Church. The one Body of Christ, composed of various local congregations and fellowships, walking, working and fellowshiping together—it is quite a sight to behold! These are cities being cared for by all the pastors and their various congregations. In some cases pastors sign public proclamations stating their intent to allow no disunity or division among pastoral relationships. As the walls of disunity are broken down, new walls of identity and integrity are erected, and the people of the city begin to see the Church through the eyes of the Lord. Such local churches then minister freely to each other's needs.

Are we prepared to reach out to that church fellowship next door?

The Legal Door

A second door concerns the legal area of the city. This includes the police, lawyers, judges and anyone responsible to care for the security of others.

I attended a conference in Virginia (1999) at which it was reported that in Baltimore the police department has a number of Christians who have formed a police intercessory unit. The police chief of that city, I heard, holds a weekly Bible study, and some of the officers have organized a praise and worship choir.

Imagine church and police intercessors ministering together in areas of social need and dysfunction in the city streets, gradually bringing transformation to the city by adopting one block at a time. Imagine a city, *your* city, in which every person and institution of the legal department is being prayed for faithfully and regularly. Think of the impact of such an investment of prayer!

The Education Door

A third door represents the educational arena. Some churches are adopting entire schools and colleges for prayer, asking God's protection and direction in the lives of students and staff alike. Such tenacious prayer is powerful! In some schools, prayer rooms have now opened as a result, and teachers and students meet for prayer early in the morning. In some places salvations and healings are occurring regularly.

The enemy regularly targets education. So must the Church!

The Commerce and Business Door

A fourth door is the business community. Again, when local churches adopt businesses for prayer, asking for God's wisdom and protection over local business people, that community is placed in an enviable position before the Lord! Many testimonies of God's direction and blessing are already being given of what happens once the Church prays strategically for this important door into the community.

It is quite a partnership when the Church and industry work together on the front line! Which business in *your* area is waiting to be adopted by *your* church?

The Political Door

A fifth door opens into the political arena. City officials require our prayers as much as anyone else; even Hezekiah gathered them together (see 2 Chronicles 29:20)! By adopting every person in local government for protection and prayer, and asking for God's wisdom and direction for that person's work, exciting spiritual breakthroughs are taking place. In every case intercessors and church leaders are caring for the city, praying any defilement and impediment out of that place.

Since we are instructed to pray for those in authority over us, let's mean business in this arena, roll up our sleeves and adopt a politician!

The Door of Influence

A final door involves people of influence. These include people such as sports figures, radio and television personalities and regular media. To pray in such a way as to bless each one, by name, and to show them your care and concern, has resulted in extraordinary breakthroughs. These people, in turn, become powerful stewards of the Kingdom, opening new doors of influence. Let's ask the Lord for His assignment of prayers in this powerful project.

Releasing Heaven on Earth

After all the work was completed and the Temple of the Lord was purified, "Hezekiah and all the people rejoiced at what God had brought about for His people, because it was done so quickly" (2 Chronicles 29:36).

The rapid completion of God's work of restoration and purification is a reflection of His call to the city and to His people today. We live in exciting days and serve an exciting God.

241

The cleansing, redemption and healing of the land, facilitating the transformation of communities and the blessing of God for His people, is what faithful stewardship is all about. It can even be termed a reflection of heaven on earth. Are we not, after all, to be praying in this manner: "Your kingdom come, your will be done on earth as it is in heaven" (Matthew 6:10)?

May we never see our communities, cities and nations in the same way again, and may God give us His revelation so that we see and plan things that reflect His heart. Even now Jesus is standing at the door of our communities and cities and nations, knocking. "If anyone hears my voice and opens the door, I will come in and eat with him, and he with me" (Revelation 3:20).

Micah 6:9 exhorts us, "Listen! The LORD is calling to the city." We must answer the call.

We live in a day of extraordinary technology, a time in which many of the secrets of life have been uncovered. Indeed, we have entered a time in history when modern science experiments not only on crops and animals, but on human beings. How far can we go?

On the first Sunday of 2000, I attended our home church service, at which time the pastor recounted this story as part of his sermon:

> In keeping with the age in which we live, a group of scientists got together one day and decided that human beings had come a long way and no longer needed God. So they picked one scientist to go and tell God.
>
> The scientist walked up to God and said, "God, we've decided we no longer need You. We are at a point where we can clone people and do many other miraculous things, so why don't You just go on and get lost?"
>
> God said, "Very well, how about this? Let's say we have a man-making contest."
>
> The scientist replied, "O.K., great!"
>
> "But," God added, "we're going to do it just as I did back in the old days with Adam."

"Sure," said the scientist, "no problem." And he bent down and grabbed himself a handful of dirt.

God looked at him and said, "No, no, you go get your own dirt."

We must not forget that God is the potter and we are the clay. He is the landlord and we are the stewards.

In this book we have looked at some biblical principles of stewardship that, when applied with prayer and diligence, will release the power of the Kingdom of heaven on earth and will prepare the way for the return of the Bridegroom. There are biblical parameters we must respect if we are to experience God's glory in our lives, in our communities, in our nations—indeed, upon our land. But first we need to recall from Joel 2:18 that the God of all creation "will be jealous for his land and take pity on his people."

> The earth is the LORD's and everything in it, the world, and all who live in it.
>
> Psalm 24:1

Amen!

Notes

Chapter 1: The Call to Be Stewards

1. Thomas Kelshaw, *Three Streams, One River: A Biblical Understanding of Stewardship* (Office of Stewardship/Development, Episcopal Church, 1985), p. 12.

2. Ibid., p. 12.

3. Ibid., p. 13.

4. Bruce C. Birch, *Economics and Faith in Biblical Perspective* (New York: Commission on Stewardship, National Council of Churches of Christ in the U.S.A., 1985), p. 3.

5. Douglas John Hall, *The Steward: A Biblical Symbol Come of Age* (Grand Rapids: Eerdmans; New York: Friendship, 1990), p. 9.

6. Ibid., p. 12.

7. Ibid., p. 23.

8. Ibid., pp. 31–32.

9. Loren Wilkinson, *Earthkeeping in the Nineties: Stewardship of Creation*, rev. ed. (Grand Rapids: Eerdmans, 1980, 1991), p. 12.

10. Ibid., p. 12.

11. Ibid., p. 16.

Chapter 2: God's Perspective on Land

1. Bob Beckett with Rebecca Wagner Sytsema, *Commitment to Conquer* (Grand Rapids: Chosen, 1997), p. 47.

2. Ibid., p. 53.

3. Winkie Pratney, *Healing the Land: A Supernatural View of Ecology* (Grand Rapids: Chosen, 1993), pp. 225–226.

4. Walter Brueggemann, *The Land* (Philadephia: Fortress, 1977), p. 96.

5. Ibid., p. 78.

6. Ibid., p. 93.

7. Ibid., p. 61.

8. Ibid., p. 60.

9. Rudy Pohl and Marny Pohl, *A Matter of the Heart: Healing Canada's Wounds* (Belleville, Ont.: Essence, 1998), p. 35.

10. Beckett & Sytsema, *Commitment*, p. 53.

11. Pratney, *Healing*, p. 131.

12. Ibid.

13. George Otis Jr., *The Twilight Labyrinth* (Grand Rapids: Chosen, 1997), p. 68.

14. Beckett & Sytsema, *Commitment*, p. 84.

15. John Dawson, *Taking Our Cities for God* (Lake Mary, Fla.: Creation House, 1989), p. 39.

16. Robert C. Linthicum, *City of God, City of Satan* (Grand Rapids: Zondervan, 1991), p. 21.

17. Ibid., p. 21.

18. Ibid., p. 25.

Chapter 3: Seeing and Believing: Our Worldview and Perspective on Land

1. Alan Richardson, ed., *A Dictionary of Christian Theology* (London: SCM, 1969), p. 334.

2. Ibid., p. 89.

3. Pohl & Pohl, *Matter*, p. 31.

4. Pratney, *Healing*, p. 142.

5. Ibid., p. 146.

6. Ibid., p. 143.

7. Ibid., p. 147.

8. Thomas B. White, *The Believer's Guide to Spiritual Warfare* (Ann Arbor, Mich.: Servant, 1990), p. 20.

9. Ibid., p. 34.

10. Ed Murphy, *The Handbook for Spiritual Warfare* (Nashville: Thomas Nelson, 1992), p. 406.

11. Clinton E. Arnold, *Ephesians' Power and Magic* (Grand Rapids: Baker, 1992), p. 65.

12. Ibid., p. 65.

13. White, *Believer's Guide*, p. 34.

14. Arnold, *Ephesians*, p. 68.

15. Murphy, *Handbook*, p. 206.

16. Walter Wink, *Naming the Powers: The Language of Power in the New Testament* (Philadelphia: Fortress, 1984), p. 85.

17. C. Peter Wagner, *Warfare Prayer* (Ventura, Calif.: Regal, 1992), p. 96.

Chapter 4: Strongholds and Stewardship

1. *New Webster's Dictionary and Thesaurus* (Danbury, Conn.: Lexicon, 1992), p. 982.

2. Ed Silvoso, *That None Should Perish* (Ventura, Calif.: Regal, 1994), p. 154.

3. Cindy Jacobs, *Possessing the Gates of the Enemy* (Tarrytown, N.Y.: Chosen, 1991), p. 100.

4. Tom White, *Breaking Strongholds* (Ann Arbor, Mich.: Servant, 1993), p. 24.

5. C. Peter Wagner, ed., *Breaking Strongholds in Your City* (Ventura, Calif.: Regal, 1993), pp. 239–240.

6. George Otis Jr., *Glossary of Related Terms with Regard to Spiritual Mapping and Spiritual Warfare* (Lynnwood, Wash.: Sentinel, 1994).

7. George Otis Jr. with Mark Brockman, eds., *Strongholds of the 10/40 Window* (Seattle: YWAM, 1995), p. 11.

8. Otis, *Twilight*, p. 200.

9. Ibid., p. 201.

10. Ibid., p. 203.

11. George Arthur Buttrick, ed., *Interpreter's Dictionary of the Bible* (Nashville: Abingdon, 1962), p. 631.

12. Ibid., p. 321.

13. Ibid., p. 631.

14. J. D. Douglas, ed., *The New Bible Dictionary* (Grand Rapids: Eerdmans, 1973), p. 1220.

15. Ibid., p. 436.

16. The name and location of this church are not identified in order to respect the privacy of its members, both past and present.

17. *New Webster's Dictionary*, p. 158.

18. Stuart Piggot, *The Druids* (London: Thames & Hudson, 1961), p. 115, quoted by Otis, *Twilight*, p. 171.

19. David Burnett, *Dawning of the Pagan Moon* (Eastbourne, E. Sussex, U.K.: Monarch, 1991), pp. 19–20.

20. Otis, *Twilight*, pp. 179–180.

21. Burnett, *Dawning*, pp. 20–21.

22. Alexander Cruden, *Cruden's Complete Concordance to the Old and New Testaments* (Toronto: G. R. Welch, 1971), p. 290.

23. Pratney, *Healing*, pp. 16–17.

Chapter 5: Past and Present: Our Spiritual DNA

1. Beckett & Sytsema, *Commitment*, pp. 49–50.

2. George Otis Jr., *The Last of the Giants* (Tarrytown, N.Y.: Chosen, 1991), p. 92.

3. Ibid.

4. John Dawson, *Healing America's Wounds* (Ventura, Calif.: Regal, 1994), p. 34.

5. Linthicum, *City of God*, p. 77.

6. Ibid., pp. 62–63.

7. Ibid., pp. 65–66.

8. Dawson, *Taking Our Cities*, p. 39.

Chapter 6: The Curse on the Land

1. Frank Hammond and Ida Mae Hammond, *The Breaking of Curses* (Plainview, Tex.: Impact, 1993), p. 3.

2. Ibid.

3. Beckett & Sytsema, *Commitment*, p. 102.

4. Ibid., p. 106.

5. C. Peter Wagner, *Lighting the World*, Book 2 in *The Acts of the Holy Spirit* series (Ventura, Calif.: Regal, 1995), p. 243.

6. Matthew Poole, *A Commentary on the Whole Bible*, Vol. 3 (London: Banner of Truth, 1969), p. 435.

7. Ron Carlson and Ed Decker, *Fast Facts on False Teachings* (Eugene, Ore.: Harvest House, 1994), p. 73.

8. Jack Harris, *Freemasonry* (New Kensington, Pa.: Whitaker, 1983), p. 13.

9. Albert Mackey, *Encyclopedia of Freemasonry*, quoted in Harris, *Freemasonry*, p. 47.

10. Albert Pike, *Morals and Dogma* (New York: H. Macoy, 1878), pp. 213–214.

11. Albert Mackey, *Encyclopedia of Freemasonry* (Philadelphia: McClure, 1924), p. 781.

12. Ibid., p. 71.

13. Otis, *Glossary*.

14. J. Havelock Fidler, *Ley Lines: Their Nature and Properties* (Welling-borough, Northamptonshire, U.K.: Turnstone, 1983), p. 32.

15. Ibid., pp. 89–90.

16. Otis, *Twilight*, p. 201.

Chapter 7: Taking Responsibility

1. Eugene H. Peterson, *Run with the Horses* (Downers Grove, Ill.: InterVarsity, 1983), pp. 61–62, quoted by Linthicum, *City of God*, p. 58.

2. Linthicum, *City of God*, p. 59.

3. Jimmie and Carol Owens, *Heal Our Land* (Grand Rapids: Revell, 1997), p. 81.

4. Ibid., p. 98.

5. Ibid., p. 99.

6. Dawson, *Wounds*, p. 90.

7. Ibid., p. 93.

8. Gary D. Kinnaman, *Overcoming the Dominion of Darkness* (Old Tappan, N.J.: Chosen, 1990), pp. 162–163.

9. Jacobs, *Possessing*, p. 111.

10. Jack Hayford, gen. ed., *The Spirit-Filled Life Bible* (Nashville: Thomas Nelson, 1991), p. 221.

Chapter 8: Stewards of the Land and City

1. Linthicum, *City of God*, pp. 98–99.

2. Ibid., p. 65–66.

3. Emeka Nwankpa, *Redeeming the Land* (Achimota, Ghana: African Christian, 1994), pp. 19–20.

4. Ibid., p. 21.

Chapter 9: With Unveiled Eyes

1. Beckett & Sytsema, *Commitment*, p. 137.

2. Ibid., p. 142.

3. Ibid., pp. 159–160.

4. Otis, *Twilight*, p. 298.

5. *Transformations* video (Lynnwood, Wash.: Sentinel, 1998).

6. Wilkinson, *Earthkeeping*, p. 310.

7. Hall, *The Steward*, p. 38.

BIBLIOGRAPHY

Arnold, Clinton E. *Ephesians' Power and Magic*. Grand Rapids: Baker Book House, 1992.

Beckett, Bob, with Rebecca Wagner Sytsema. *Commitment to Conquer*. Grand Rapids: Chosen, 1997.

Birch, Bruce C. *Economics and Faith in Biblical Perspective*. New York: Commission on Stewardship, National Council of Churches of Christ in the U.S.A., 1985.

Brueggemann, Walter. *The Land*. Philadelphia: Fortress, 1977.

Burnett, David. *Dawning of the Pagan Moon*. Eastbourne, E. Sussex, U.K.: Monarch, 1991.

Buttrick, George Arthur, ed. *Interpreter's Dictionary of the Bible*. Nashville: Abingdon, 1962.

Carlson, Ron, and Ed Decker. *Fast Facts on False Teachings*. Eugene, Ore.: Harvest House, 1994.

Concise Oxford Dictionary. London: Oxford University, 1964.

Cruden, Alexander. *Cruden's Complete Concordance to the Old and New Testaments*. Toronto: G. R. Welch, 1971.

Dawson, John. *Healing America's Wounds*. Ventura, Calif.: Regal, 1994.

_____. *Taking Our Cities for God*. Lake Mary, Fla.: Creation House, 1989.

Encyclopedia Brittanica, Vol. 10. London: William Benton, 1981.

Fidler, J. Havelock. *Ley Lines: Their Nature and Properties*. Wellingborough, Northamptonshire, U.K.: Turnstone, 1983.

Hall, Douglas John. *The Steward: A Biblical Symbol Come of Age*. New York: Friendship, and Grand Rapids: Eerdmans, 1990.

Hammond, Frank, and Ida Mae Hammond. *The Breaking of Curses*. Plainview, Tex.: Impact, 1993.

Harris, Jack. *Freemasonry*. New Kensington, Pa.: Whitaker House, 1983.

Jacobs, Cindy. *Possessing the Gates of the Enemy*. Tarrytown, N.Y.: Chosen, 1991.

Kelshaw, Thomas. *Three Streams, One River: A Biblical Understanding of Stewardship*. The Office of Stewardship/Development, Episcopal Church, 1985.

Linthicum, Robert C. *City of God, City of Satan*. Grand Rapids: Zondervan, 1991.

Mackey, Albert. *Encyclopedia of Freemasonry*. Philadelphia: McClure, 1924.

Murphy, Ed. *The Handbook for Spiritual Warfare*. Nashville: Thomas Nelson, 1992.

Nwankpa, Emeka. *Redeeming the Land*. Achimota, Ghana. African Christian, 1994.

Otis, George Jr. *Glossary of Related Terms with Regard to Spiritual Mapping and Spiritual Warfare*. Lynnwood, Wash.: Sentinel, 1994.

_____. *The Last of the Giants*. Tarrytown, N.Y.: Chosen, 1991.

_____. *The Twilight Labyrinth*. Grand Rapids: Chosen, 1997.

_____ with Mark Brockman, eds. *Strongholds of the 10/40 Window*. Seattle: YWAM, 1995.

Owens, Jimmy, and Carol Owens. *Heal Our Land*. Grand Rapids: Revell, 1997.

Peterson, Eugene. *Run with the Horses*. Downers Grove, Ill.: InterVarsity, 1983.

Pike, Albert. *Morals and Dogma*. New York: H. Macoy, 1878.

Pohl, Rudy, and Marny Pohl. *A Matter of the Heart: Healing Canada's Wounds*. Belleville, Ont.: Essence, 1998.

Poole, Matthew. *A Commentary on the Whole Bible*, Vol. 3. London: Banner of Truth, 1969.

Pratney, Winkie. *Healing the Land: A Supernatural View of Ecology*. Grand Rapids: Chosen, 1993.

Richardson, Alan, ed. *A Dictionary of Christian Theology*. London: SCM, 1969.

Silvoso, Edgardo. *That None Should Perish*. Ventura, Calif.: Regal, 1994.

Wagner, C. Peter., ed. *Breaking Strongholds in Your City.* Ventura, Calif.: Regal, 1993.

_____. *Lighting the World*. Book 2, *The Acts of the Holy Spirit* series. Ventura, Calif.: Regal, 1995.

_____. *Warfare Prayer*. Ventura, Calif.: Regal, 1992.

New Webster's Dictionary and Thesaurus of the English Language. Danbury, Conn.: Lexicon, 1992.

Webster's New World Dictionary, 2nd college edition, 1978.

White, Thomas B. *The Believer's Guide to Spiritual Warfare*. Ann Arbor, Mich.: Servant, 1990.

_____. *Breaking Strongholds*. Ann Arbor, Mich.: Servant, 1993.

Wilkinson, Loren. *Earthkeeping in the Nineties: Stewardship of Creation*, rev. ed. Grand Rapids: Eerdmans, 1980.

Wink, Walter. *Naming the Powers: The Language of Power in the New Testament*. Philadelphia: Fortress, 1984.

Scripture Index

Genesis

1:4   109
1:10   109, 146, 236
1:12   109
1:18   109
1:21   109
1:25   109
1:26   25, 33
1:28   21, 26, 33
1:31   109
2:7   109
2:9   153
2:15   22, 26, 146
3   81, 153
3:14   143
3:17   42, 143
3:18–19   42
4   42
4:7   175
4:8   39
4:11–12   42
4:12   39
4:16   39
9:19   35
10:20   35
10:31   35
11   153
11:8–9   35
12:1–3   93

Exodus

6:9   106
16:4–5   24
19:5   226

19:5–6   40
20:3–4   58
20:5   58
20:6   58
23:10–13   66
24   63
30   196
30:22–25   195
30:31–33   195
32   65

Leviticus

2:13   192
3:17   149
11:44   175
11:44–45   98
17:11   198
18:1–23   59
18:22   60
18:24–25   43, 60
18:24–28   100
18:25   200
18:25–28   145
18:26–27   220
18:27–28   43
19:29   43, 60
20   41
20:22–24   175
20:23–24   41
20:26   96
23:21   130
25:23   22
25:24   110
25:24–25   95
26   232

26:4–10   200
26:5   201
26:6   201
26:7–8   201
26:9   201
26:10   201
26:11–13   201
26:14–39   65
26:34–35   65
26:39   39
26:39–42   39
26:40–41   66
26:40–42   101
26:42–43   66

Numbers

13:23–24   43
13:28   106
13:31   107
13:33   107
16   181
16:46   181
16:48   181
18:19   192
35:33   145, 172, 182, 199
35:33–34   61

Deuteronomy

5:7–9   176
5:7–10   40
5:9   40, 121
7   108
7:6   40, 145, 176
7:16   108

257

Subject Index

accountability, 57, 59
adamh.
　See land: biblical words
agnosticism, 56
agros.
　See land: biblical words
animism, 103
anointing oil, 195–98
Arnold, Clinton, 77;
　Ephesians' Power and Magic, 77
atheism, 56
authorities (*exousia*), 74, 75, 76, 78

Bali prayer initiative, 163–66
Beckett, Bob, 31, 42, 46, 115, 144, 229–30;
　Commitment to Conquer, 31, 144
binding and loosing, 189–90
Birch, Bruce C., 25–26
bloodshed, 61–62;
　suicide, 43
bondage:
　breaking of, 188–90;
　formula of, 119–20;
　residence of wounds, 120–22;
　shaped by stewardship, 122–26
Brockman, Mark, 84;

Strongholds of the 10/40 Window, 84
Brueggemann, Walter, 33–34, 35;
　The Land, 33–34
Burnett, David, 103, 104;
　Dawning of the Pagan Moon, 103

Carlson, Ron, 151;
　Fast Facts on False Teachings, 151
Celtic spiritual history, 102–3
chora.
　See land: biblical words
chorion.
　See land: biblical words
cities, 49–50, 209–26
cleansing:
　elements of spiritual, 190–200.
　See also anointing oil; Holy Communion; salt; water
climate:
　spiritual, 38
commission:
　Paul's, 54
communities:
　transformed, 228–32, 235
confession:
　and forgiveness, 187–88

consecration:
　of self, 180–82
covenant, 108;
　broken, 62–64;
　New, 186–87;
　renewed in Jesus, 63
culture:
　influence of, 129–32;
　and neutralized characteristics of, 130;
　settings, 94–95
curses:
　issue of, 141–43;
　recognizing, 150

Dawson, John, 46, 47, 132, 187;
　Healing America's Wounds, 132;
　Taking Our Cities for God, 46, 135
Decker, Ed, 151;
　Fast Facts on False Teachings, 151
defilement:
　four causes of, 57–64, 173;
　and land connections, 65–67;
　Scriptural examples of, 42–44.
　See also land: and defilement; stewards: and defilement
deism, 55–56, 59
demonic activity, 42, 188.

orn in Scotland and raised in Canada, Alistair P. Petrie found his first career in Canadian broadcasting. He later undertook training for the ministry in London and was ordained into the Anglican Church in York, England, in 1976. He has since ministered in parishes in both England and Scotland, as well as in his most recent position as rector of Brentwood Anglican Chapel, Brentwood Bay, British Columbia, for more than fifteen years. He received the D.Min. degree from Fuller Theological Seminary in the area of Spiritual Issues in Church Growth.

Alistair has been a proponent of renewal and evangelism in the Anglican/Episcopal Church for many years, and has been involved in conference and mission work as a plenary speaker and workshop leader throughout North America and overseas. He is also a regular teacher with various parachurch ministries. Alistair is involved with a number of the prayer initiatives currently being undertaken in many parts of the 10/40 Window.

Alistair is the Canadian coordinator for the Spiritual Warfare Network, part of the networking structure of the A.D. 2000 United Prayer Track. His main thrust of ministry in recent years has been in helping the Church discover the cutting-edge insights of turning an entire community toward Christ. He gives instruction in the biblical understanding of the stewardship of land and the effect this has on people, churches, communities and cities. Through this teaching it becomes possible through historical, cultural, physical and spiritual research to diagnose the bondages and wounds in an area that often impede effective evangelism. Alistair has developed this teaching utilizing the tools of intercession, spiritual warfare, spiritual mapping and commitment to the land as essential components in liberating and transforming a community into Christ.

Alistair left residential ministry in June 1997 to devote full time to his work as director of Joshua Connection Canada, an interdenominational enabling and mission ministry that serves the broader Body of Christ throughout North America and overseas. He is also the executive director of Sentinel Ministries Canada; the director of International Operations for The Sentinel Group; the present chaplain to the board of March for Jesus, Canada; and a member of the board of Every Home for Christ International/Canada. Alistair also serves as the Canadian representative on the international board of the World Prayer Center in Colorado Springs.

He is married to Marie and they have two sons, Michael and Richard.